About This Book

Why is this topic important?

As the complexity of the issues we must solve multiplies from one day to the next, our successes as members of teams increasingly depends on our ability to share information, solve problems, collaborate, and play intentionally to each other's strengths. *Games That Boost Performance* tackles head-on the challenge of how we progress from being strong individual contributors to being effective team members. While the content of the games can easily be adapted to any industry, profession, or topic, the underlying themes of all these games reinforce the importance of learning to work together in order to achieve our goals. Boosting performance is not simply a matter of adequate capitalization, good leadership, or reliable infrastructure. Improved performance rests on the ability of every team to boost the performance of its individual members and its performance as a collective unit.

What can you achieve with this book?

This book serves as both a working reference and a valuable source of games that focus teams on the factors that will enable them to succeed—regardless of the goal, regardless of the time frame. In the first part of the book, the authors create a foundation for thinking about the issues that confront all teams and the skills that facilitators need to be able to guide discussion of those issues. What follows—the heart of the book—are thirty games, set-up instructions, and discussion notes that will enable the novice or experienced facilitator to lead effective team-building exercises.

How is this book organized?

The Introduction lays out some basic rules for success in using games to teach and outlines thirteen performance improvement goals common to most teams—these include coaching, collaboration, communication, creativity, feedback, goal definition, planning/strategy, role definition, tapping team resources, values/culture, and working with information. A matrix shows which games link to which team-building goals. The games can be used to enhance team problem-solving skills by highlighting how we go about defining a problem, brainstorming alternatives, thinking laterally, and developing strategies. They can be used to surface and compare deeply held values, to explore the conditions under which teams choose to compete or collaborate, and to make manifest the "myths" individuals hold about their organizations. Each game describes the purpose, ideal audience size, rules of play, instructions, facilitator notes, timing, and worksheets or templates, as appropriate.

About Pfeiffer

Pfeiffer serves the professional development and hands-on resource needs of training and human resource practitioners and gives them products to do their jobs better. We deliver proven ideas and solutions from experts in HR development and HR management, and we offer effective and customizable tools to improve workplace performance. From novice to seasoned professional, Pfeiffer is the source you can trust to make yourself and your organization more successful.

Essential Knowledge Pfeiffer produces insightful, practical, and comprehensive materials on topics that matter the most to training and HR professionals. Our Essential Knowledge resources translate the expertise of seasoned professionals into practical, how-to guidance on critical workplace issues and problems. These resources are supported by case studies, worksheets, and job aids and are frequently supplemented with CD-ROMs, websites, and other means of making the content easier to read, understand, and use.

Essential Tools Pfeiffer's Essential Tools resources save time and expense by offering proven, ready-to-use materials—including exercises, activities, games, instruments, and assessments—for use during a training or team-learning event. These resources are frequently offered in looseleaf or CD-ROM format to facilitate copying and customization of the material.

Pfeiffer also recognizes the remarkable power of new technologies in expanding the reach and effectiveness of training. While e-hype has often created whizbang solutions in search of a problem, we are dedicated to bringing convenience and enhancements to proven training solutions. All our e-tools comply with rigorous functionality standards. The most appropriate technology wrapped around essential content yields the perfect solution for today's on-the-go trainers and human resource professionals.

Pfeiffer
www.pfeiffer.com   *Essential resources for training and HR professionals*

Games That Boost Performance

STEVE SUGAR AND CAROL WILLETT

Pfeiffer
A Wiley Imprint
www.pfeiffer.com

Published by Pfeiffer
An Imprint of Wiley.
989 Market Street, San Francisco, CA 94103-1741 www.pfeiffer.com

ISBN: 0-7879-7135-9

Library of Congress Cataloging-in-Publication Data
Sugar, Steve.
  Games that boost performance / Steve Sugar and Carol Willett.
    p. cm.
  ISBN 0-7879-7135-9 (alk. paper)
  1. Management games.   2. Achievement motivation.   3. Organizational effectiveness.
  4. Organizational learning.   5. Performance.   6. Employees—Training of.
  I. Willett, Carol   II. Title.
    HD30.26.S837 2005
    658.4'0353—dc22
                                                                                    2004006378

Acquiring Editor: *Martin Delahoussaye*
Director of Development: *Kathleen Dolan Davies*
Developmental Editor: *Susan Rachmeler*
Production Editor: *Nina Kreiden*
Editor: *Rebecca Taff*
Manufacturing Supervisor: *Bill Matherly*
Editorial Assistant: *Laura Reizman*
Illustrations: *Interactive Composition Corporation*

Printed in the United States of America

Printing   10   9   8   7   6   5   4   3   2   1

Dedications

· ·

If a writer of games is first a child and second a writer, then pity
my poor family, especially my wife, Marie.

To my grandchildren—Clarisse, Luke, Quinn, Dillon, and
Jack—whose delightful adventures remind me that all learning
should be a path of joyful discovery.

To Martin Delahoussaye for his encouragement and support
throughout the project.

Steve Sugar

To my son, Adam, and my husband, Richard, who have taught me
the critical importance and utter seriousness of play. Without them,
I would have indeed become a dull girl.

Carol Willett

Contents

Contents of the CD-ROM

• •

CLUE LESS

Player Instructions

Time Card

Master Time Card

Additional Scenario

COUNTER INTELLIGENCE

Player Instructions

Game Sheet

DOUBLE PLAY

Player Instructions

Worksheet

Sample Word Changes

DRAGON SQUARES

Player Instructions
Game Sheet

FLOOR PLAN

Player Instructions

Planner Instruction Sheet

Floor Manager Instruction Sheet

Floor Team Instruction Sheet

Directions Sheet

Solution Sheets

FLOOR TEAMS

Player Instructions

Floor Team X Instructions

Floor Team O Instructions

Planning Grid

Solution Sheets

FRIENDLY PERSUASION

Player Instructions

Award Criteria

GHOSTWRITER

Player Instructions

Ballot Sheets

HARD CASE

Player Instructions

Game Chart

Answer Sheets

Sample Case Study

HAVING A BAD HAIR DAY

Player Instructions

List of Annoying Events

THE HELLO EFFECT

Player Instructions

Mood Cards

Response Sheets

IMPROBABLE HEADLINES

Player Instructions

Samples

INITIAL ASSUMPTIONS

Player Instructions

Sample Puzzle Sheet

Puzzle Sheets

LISTEN UP

Player Instructions

Sample I

Sample II

Team Worksheet

NEWSCAST

Player Instructions

Guidelines

Presentation Ballot

Sample Case

Introduction

· ·

Getting the Most from This Resource

When is a game more than a game? When you use it as a jumping-off point for discussing the assumptions we make and the tactics we typically employ in working with others. On one level the games in this book can be used to orient new hires to the organizational culture they have just entered, to reinforce learning on virtually any subject matter or interest, or to break the ice with a newly formed group. We guarantee that the games will work just fine to accomplish those goals.

At a deeper level these games can also be used to probe other dimensions of team performance. As you debrief these games you can provoke significant discussions about the assumptions we make about a task, about each other, and about our appropriate roles. You can use them to enhance team problem-solving skills by highlighting how we go about defining a problem, brainstorming alternatives, thinking laterally, and developing strategies. You can use them as a means to surface and compare deeply held values, to explore the conditions under which we choose to compete or collaborate, and to investigate the assumptions we hold about our organizations.

Games can evoke powerful learning—not only by reinforcing the right answer, but also by exploring the process by which a team or individual defines the problem, describes the goal, identifies assumptions, and generates alternatives. The learning moment—both when you are acknowledged as having the "right" answer as well as when you gain insight into how you think and problem solve—occurs over and over. Experiential learning occurs both while playing the game and later as we think about what we learned. Your ability to apply games that evoke this powerful learning depends on both your knowledge of the subject matter and your knowledge of your audience.

Games That Boost Performance can be used on many levels to physically—as well as mentally—engage people in the process of defining what it means to "win" and how best to achieve that end. We believe that the book's value lies in the fact that—just as in the workplace—things are rarely as simple as they may appear. Any of these games can be used to attain the stated primary objective. They can also be used as a catalyst to spur your own thinking about the links between game behavior and how we typically interact with team members in the "real world."

In creating this book, the authors merged two very different, but complementary perspectives.

- Steve Sugar is a Game-Meister who excels at creating "game frames." His imagination is sparked by the challenge of creating the *melody* of the game—establishing the character of the game and then defining the rules of play and developing the guidelines for scoring. Steve has a gift for making learning kinesthetic by turning acts of mental recall into physical competitions that trigger the adrenaline and create the sense of immediacy and purpose that drives deep learning.

- Carol Willett is a team facilitator who excels at scripting facilitation. Her input will help you apply each of these games to specific organization development challenges. Carol's post-game debriefing questions and comments create the *lyrics* for the game. It is through debriefing that you help participants to understand the dynamics of team performance and see how to apply their lessons learned back to the workplace.

● ENGAGING GRIM GROWNUPS

The workplace today is not one where "gaming" has very good connotations. Most of us take a serious (if not grim) attitude toward the business of earning our living and the prospect of "playing a game" in order to learn is not one that is immediately inviting for much of the workforce. Despite what we know about the benefits of experiential learning, the value of practice rather than lecture, and the long-term retention of learning that comes from active participation, there is a residual wariness about using games to boost team performance. Here are three rules for engaging grim grown-ups:

Rule 1: Connect the Dots. Begin with the organizational challenge or task—people want to know how what they are about to do connects with their world of work, their day-to-day concerns, or the expectations the organization has of them. It takes less time for people to "connect the dots" between their work and the game you are about to introduce if you begin with one or more of the following questions:

- When you or your team is asked to analyze a solution, generate options, or choose a strategy, what is the hardest part of getting started?

- As you think about the teams in which you have been a member, what are some of the typical pitfalls, roadblocks, or barriers that they encountered?

- If you could do just one or two things to improve your own or your team's performance, what would they be?

Rule 2: Select the Right Game.   There is no one game or one experience that can adequately or even partially serve all purposes. The game matrix, found on page 8, suggests which games are best-suited for specific learning purposes. The post-game debriefing questions and notes that accompany each game will help you think through what you are specifically trying to achieve and help you tailor your processing questions to elicit the learning that you think is most important.

Rule 3: Carefully Name the Experience.   Don't call the interaction a "game"— you will have less resistance by introducing it as a "practical application," a "team challenge," an "exercise," or an "experience."

● IDENTIFY PERFORMANCE-IMPROVEMENT GOALS

Finding the right game begins with needs analysis. What is the problem you are trying to address or the area of performance you would like to improve? It is important to establish a set of learning objectives—what you want your audience to learn or demonstrate. Then you can evaluate how well the game met your expectations.

How do you improve team performance? There are many ways of doing this, but this book focuses on thirteen key variables that, in our experience, lend themselves to games. Each of the terms defined below supports one or more aspects of effective team performance that will surface in one or more of the thirty games described in this book. While these terms may have different meanings in different contexts—a football coach and an opera coach bring somewhat different knowledge, skills, and abilities to their professions—we have defined these terms from the perspective of improving individual or team performance. Our definitions are utterly idiosyncratic and may not conform to what you would read in Webster's dictionary, but we can vouch for the fact that these issues will surface naturally, and sometimes dramatically, as you play and process these games. We hope that the definitions will enable you to more easily match games to specific audience needs or performance-improvement goals.

Coaching.   Coaching includes the following behaviors:

- Calling individual or group attention to what is happening in the moment.

- Prompting people to consider whether what they are doing is effective or ineffective. As my P.E. teacher remarked during the archery module, "Your chances of hitting the target would improve dramatically if you didn't shut your eyes and cringe when you release the arrow."

- Reminding an individual or group of the need to play to identified resources, talents, or strengths.

- Providing real-time feedback on whether an individual or group is moving closer to or away from stated goals or objectives.

Collaboration.   Collaboration includes the following behaviors:

- Identifying the interests, equities, and "stake" held by others in this situation. Most "teams" assume they are in a competitive situation unless they are specifically told otherwise and tend to define interactions with other teams as "win/lose" propositions or zero-sum games.

- Identifying the information, talent, or resources that the team and others can contribute to achieving shared or compatible goals.

- Negotiating expectations and protocols for interaction and information sharing such that both parties are able to succeed in completing their assigned tasks.

Communication.   Communication includes the following behaviors:

- Clearly and accurately conveying the information that is known to the individual or team.

- Identifying what is unknown, unavailable, or missing.

- Sharing tacit (generally unspoken) assumptions about the problem, the situation, information one has, the resources available, and so forth.

- Providing feedback on the impact of decisions or actions made by others.

- Asking questions, listening carefully, and seeking clarification as needed.

Creativity.   Creativity includes the following behaviors:

- Questioning one's assumptions about the problem, the situation, the rules or constraints, and the information or options available.

- Reframing problems in such a way that you consider a wide range of alternatives and many categories of possible solutions.

- Generating a volume of ideas before narrowing the scope down to a handful of possible strategies or options.

- The ability to define a problem from multiple perspectives.

- The ability to engage in lateral thinking and ask questions in a way that helps to solve the problem at hand.

Feedback. Feedback includes providing information that:

- Tells an individual whether they succeeded or failed. This may involve simply handing out the right answer, the facilitator saying "You're RIGHT!" or "WRONG-O!" or sounding a bell, buzzer, or gong.

- Conveys the impact or consequences of a choice or an action.

- Allows an individual to modify behavior to "self-correct" in order to become more effective. For example, when you ask someone to scratch an itch between your shoulder blades, it is useful feedback to say "up and a little to the left" and then sigh "Ahhhhhhh!" when he or she hits the spot.

Goal Definition. This performance goal appears in every game.

Most of us, most of the time, fail to adequately define our goals, whether we are working as individuals or as members of a team or collaborative effort. As a result, it is easy to wander off track, to lose sight of what we are trying to achieve, or to properly prioritize our efforts. Goal definition includes the following aspects:

- Defining WHAT we are trying to achieve.

- Defining WHY it matters that we achieve it.

- Defining HOW WE WILL KNOW IF WE SUCCEED.

- Defining the CONSEQUENCES of failure.

Planning/Strategy. Planning and strategy include the following aspects:

- Identifying what critical information, actions, or choices are needed in order to succeed.

- Figuring out the shortest action path between where we are and what we want to achieve.

- Identifying the probable impact of other players and their goals on what we are trying to achieve.

- Aligning our time, information, resources, and talent in such a way that we make the best possible use of each in pursuing our goals.

Problem Solving.   Problem solving includes the following skills:

- Defining the problem. Consider the family's flooded basement. One partner defines the problem as "how to get the water out of the basement" and pays to have sump pumps installed. The other partner defines the problem as "how to keep water from getting into the basement" and installs six-inch gutters, regrades the ground away from the house, and petitions the local government to install a larger storm drain on the adjoining street. How you define a problem limits the range of solutions you choose.

- Surfacing, sharing, and challenging assumptions.

- Brainstorming possibilities.

- Developing criteria for selecting an answer.

- Weighing pros and cons.

- Choosing (and committing to) a course of action.

- Checking for feedback on whether one has made a correct choice.

Role Definition.   Role definition includes the following elements:

- What needs to be done for the team to succeed? Someone may need to keep time, interpret the rules, organize available information, divide the labor, inventory the talent, act as coach, answer the questions, make decisions, spy on what the other teams are doing, be the writer, be the briefer, or test the waters so the team can find out what's going on.

- Who is best equipped to carry out those tasks?

- What do we expect of the person who takes on this role?

- How can we help or support the person in carrying out this role effectively?

Tapping Team Resources.   Tapping team resources includes finding out:

- Who is knowledgeable about what?

- Who has experience in this or related areas?

- Who has a natural gift or ability for carrying out one or more roles or for taking on a specific responsibility?

Trust. The issue of trust usually involves:

- Establishing expectations.

- Negotiating acceptable/unacceptable behavior.

- Specifying consequences.

Values/Culture. Determining shared or conflicting values and exploring the nature and impact of team or organizational culture includes:

- Describing the rationale and motivations that underlie our behavior.

- Describing what we see happening around us and the reasons or explanations that we apply to make sense of those actions or behaviors.

- Examining the assumptions and stories we create about "why things happen."

- Looking at the image we hold about what our organization or team stands for and the values it promotes.

- Understanding the impact of the gap between "the way they tell it" and "the way it is."

Working with Information. Working with information includes:

- Doing an inventory of what is known and unknown.

- Developing a common, shared understanding of available information.

- Analyzing what is significant and what is peripheral to the matter at hand.

The following matrix will help you identify those games that primarily address one of the performance goals described above. While many of the games in this book can be used to achieve multiple goals, the matrix will help you zero in on which games address which performance issues.

● TYPICAL WORKPLACE SITUATIONS

What are some typical situations in which a game could shorten the learning curve and boost performance? Here are six workplace applications that could easily lend themselves to using games. Each situation is briefly described and then followed by a list of the games we would choose.

Games Versus Performance Matrix

Game →

Goal →	Coach	Collab	Comm	Creat	Fdbk	Pln/Str	Prob Solv	R Def	T Tm R	Trust	Val/Cult	Wk Info
Best of Wurst			x	x							Prim	
Cash Box	x	x	Prim			x	x	Prim	x			
Champions	x	x			x			x	x			Prim
Clue Less		x	x				Prim		x			x
Counter Intelligence		x	x			Prim				x		
Double Play		x	x	Prim			Prim		x			
Dragon Squares		Prim	x			x						
Floor Plan	x	Prim	x		x	Prim		x	x			
Floor Teams	x	Prim	x		x	Prim	x	x				
Friendly Persuasion		Prim	x		x	x					Prim	
Ghostwriter			x	x					x			Prim
Hard Case			x				Prim		x			x
Having Bad Hair Day		x		Prim					x		Prim	
The Hello Effect			Prim		x							
Improbable Headlines		x	x	x					x		Prim	x
Initial Assumptions		x		Prim			x		x			x
Listen Up			Prim		x		x					x
Newscast		x	x						x			Prim
Passport		x	x	x					Prim			x
Proxy	x		x		x			Prim	x			Prim
Rear View Mirror	Prim		x		x			x	x	Prim		
Sandwiches			x	Prim			x		x			
Scavenger Bingo		x		Prim			x		x			
Second Mouse						Prim	Prim			x	x	x
Smack Down				x					x			Prim
Speed Dial				x						x	Prim	
Splitting Hares			x	x	x	Prim						x
Tattoo		x	x	x							Prim	
Team Poker		Prim	x		x	x	x					x
Virtual X-Change		Prim	Prim		x		x					x

Legend

Prim = primary goal of game   x = additional goal or use of game

coach = coaching

collab = collaboration

comm = communication

creat = creativity

fdbk = feedback

pln/str = planning/strategy

prob solv = problem solving

r def = role definition

t tm r = tapping team resources

trust = trust

val/cult = values/culture

wk info = working with information

Note: Because "Goal Definition" is a goal of every game, it is not included in this matrix.

Situation #1: Icebreaker

Rather than throwing a group directly into a task, you want to introduce them to each other, "warm them up," and spark their creativity and problem-solving energy. Excellent icebreakers include:

- Having a Bad Hair Day
- Initial Assumptions
- Passport
- Sandwiches
- Scavenger Bingo

Situation #2: New Hire Orientation

Learning your way around is a critical task for new hires. To introduce people to a new culture you can use games that explore organizational values, introduce specific terminology, clarify responsibilities, or provoke discussion of "what it takes to succeed around here." Good games for this purpose include:

- Champions
- Clue Less
- Friendly Persuasion
- Ghostwriter
- Passport
- Proxy
- Tattoo

Situation #3: Fine-Tuning Team Communication and Collaboration

Sometimes it isn't what a team knows, it's how it works (or doesn't work) together. This is largely determined by how well a team defines its goals, deploys its resources, and assigns responsibility and on how effectively it is able to collaborate and problem solve. The following games speak directly to those issues:

- Cash Box
- Counter Intelligence

- Dragon Squares

- Floor Teams

- The Hello Effect

Situation #4: Focusing on Planning and Strategy

Most of us focus on the tactical, rather than the strategic. As a result it's all too easy to develop a short-term and somewhat myopic view of what needs to happen and how best to make it happen. The following games force teams to reexamine those tendencies and to develop a more rigorous approach to planning and strategy.

- Counter Intelligence

- Floor Plan

- Team Poker

- Virtual X-Change

Situation #5: Topic Review

You want to ensure that the group is operating on a common level of understanding of a given topic. It is appropriate for them to discuss how it is that group members know what they know, as well as the implications of this knowledge for a task at hand.

- Champions

- Clue Less

- Ghostwriter

- Hard Case

- Second Mouse Gets the Cheese

- Smack Down

Situation #6: Individual or Organizational Values

Knowing what attracts us, motivates us, or repels us is part of the glue that holds organizations together and enables effective group effort. Yet values—shared or otherwise—are not normal topics of team conversation or the stuff of which staff meetings are made. The following games help surface these issues in productive ways:

- Best of the Wurst
- Friendly Persuasion
- Speed Dial
- Tattoo

● SELECTING YOUR GAME

You can fine-tune your game selection skills by considering the following issues.

Audience

- Who is your audience?
- What is their level of knowledge?
- Is this their first exposure either to the organization, to their team members, or to the subject matter?
- What do they need to learn?
- Is the goal to expand their knowledge of a process or to improve their team-building skills?
- Are your participants responsible for training, coaching, or leading others and do they need to become more conscious of and proficient in the skills involved?

Number of Players

Next you need to think about the composition of your teams. Active participation on a team is an important element of the game experience. Teams not only present a collective approach to problem solving, but they are less threatened during the question-response period. If an individual responds incorrectly, he or she may feel embarrassed or stupid; if the team responds incorrectly, there is a mixed experience of both disappointment and discovery. Teams also reinforce the fact that team members can, and should, learn from one another.

The size of a good working team varies from two to seven players. Teams usually function better with an odd number of players such as three, five, or seven. Having an odd number of players produces natural tiebreakers. If possible, try to use three members on a team, unless the rules indicate otherwise. Using three players allows all players to become involved in the question responses and other aspects of game play.

The larger your group, the more carefully you will need to think through how you debrief the game. We do not just learn by doing. We learn by talking about what we have done, why we did it, and whether the outcomes were what we wanted or expected. Group discussion of what was learned is critical to effectively engaging adults in games.

Here are some strategies to ensure adequate discussion in large groups:

- Provide a discussion guide for each table or team and specify how many minutes are available for discussion.

- Ask each team or table group to answer one or two questions from the discussion guide.

- Have each group discuss the entire set of questions and then summarize and report out two key learnings from the experience.

- Have one group or a percentage of participants play the game or just one round, with the rest of the group acting as observers and reporters. If you choose this strategy, you need to clearly spell out what you want your observers to look for and how you want them to capture and report their observations. This is a significant task in and of itself, and you will need to double the discussion time to allow for observers to report.

- If you have multiple groups or teams running simultaneously, recruit some assistants! Assign them to work with individual teams to keep the effort on track, to discuss the experience, and to report out what is happening and what has been learned.

Playing Time

"How long do we have?" is always a critical issue. Game play represents only part of the total experience, which includes set-up, game play, and processing the experience and lessons learned.

Set-Up. The set-up and introduction take approximately 10 percent of your time. This involves setting up the room, distributing game materials, dividing participants into teams, and reviewing the rules of play.

Game Play.   The actual game playing experience takes approximately 50 percent of your time. This is when you start and stop play, clarify questions about the rules or content, provide correct responses, and declare winners. An easy way to time play is to use timed music sequences. You can use your own favorite musical pieces with established run times (such as minutes and seconds listed on a CD) or "game show" style music ("Offbeat Training Tunes," Millbower, www.offbeattraining.com).

Debriefing.   Facilitating the discussion of the experience requires approximately 40 percent of the time available. This is when you discover what happened, why it happened, and what people learned from their experience. When in doubt, err on the side of planning for more discussion time than you think you will need. It's through talking about what we have just done that learning "sticks."

Game Variations

Once you have selected and played a game, you may want to modify one or more of the elements. We have included suggested variations and options with each of the games based on the following factors:

- Size of group.

- Time of play.

- Method of play.

- Scoring.

● DEVELOPING GAME CONTENT

In those situations in which your specific goal is to introduce or reinforce terminology, information, policies, guidelines, or work practices, you will want the content of the game to reflect your specific organization and the ways in which you work. Your ability to match the game experience to "real life" is a function of creating questions and situations that mirror what goes on in the workplace. Here are the steps involved in tailoring game content to your purpose and goals:

1. *Review your learning objectives.* What do you want participants to learn or think about as a result of this experience?

2. *Determine the content.* To select, translate, and incorporate "real-life" content into the game frame you will want to first select information (terms, acronyms, process steps, problems, role titles, or functions) that match your

organization or work place and next, translate these items into game-sized pieces or information nuggets by using short questions, mini-case studies, or situations.

3. *Develop the questions.* With each question you should include the preferred response, the rationale (for elaboration during the answer period), and the reference source (for your own documentation and use). Since what we write is rarely as clear to others as it is to ourselves, it's prudent to "pre-test" your material on a guinea-pig group before you "go live" in the classroom with your primary audience. To do this, you may develop thirty to fifty test items or three to five case studies that embody the most important concepts and facts you want to convey. Create a conceptual flow that moves participants from least-complex issues to most-complex by placing the items in a specific order. Or you may choose a random sequence to represent the "luck of the draw" involved in game play. Assign values (points) to the questions as necessary. Assigning additional points to an important fact or concept underscores its importance. Sort the information into "critical" and "nice to have" categories. This will enable you to focus game play when time is limited or expand to take advantage of additional time.

4. *Incorporate questions into the game format.* Transfer them onto individual question cards or team worksheets. We have provided a suggested framework for those games that focus on working with information.

Question-Writing Tips

Here are some reminders when developing short information-item questions:

1. Write questions in a conversational format because game questions are usually read aloud.

2. Write closed-ended questions—questions that focus on one response. This ensures that the requested information and its rationale are covered in the question-and-response format.

3. Focus each question on one fact. This keeps the information precise and brief. If needed, use several questions to ensure that the learning concept is covered adequately.

4. Be brief. Use simple wording for both questions and answers. As a rule, questions used for reinforcement should contain fewer than thirty-five words.

5. Be prepared for the moment of learning—that moment when you have the "right" answer as well as when you gain insight into how you think and problem solve. Be able to explain why one answer is "right" or preferred over other options. Where the solution or answer is a matter of judgment, make sure you can explain the factors you considered in making that judgment.

6. Number each question. This helps you with your question count and gives you a way to quickly identify and review questions that may require adjustment, deletion, or updating.

Sample Question Formats

Variety adds challenge and a change of pace to games that focus on introducing or reinforcing information. The following types of questions help sustain interest and focus on different levels of learning from recall to pattern recognition to analysis to problem solving.

Direct Question.   Usually prompts players to recall or identify a definition, fact, person, place, or thing (Name the "find and replace" function key on your keyboard). Be sure to include enough information to allow players to provide the proper answer.

Fill-in-the-Blank.   This method requires the player to sort through a range of possible answers and select the one that best fits this context.

Multiple-Choice.   This format presents the correct response along with two distracting responses—choices a, b, or c. Since many question periods are "timed," reducing your choices to three minimizes confusion and helps speed up play.

True-False.   This is the easiest type of question to prepare and answer, and it offers players a 50/50 chance to respond correctly. Developing more than 40 percent of your questions in this format will quickly bore your audience as well as reduce the problem solution to a coin-toss.

Partial Listing.   This requires the multiple identification of items in a category or listing. This is more typically used for a written, rather than oral response. Using a "partial" list (Name three of five possible choices) underscores the importance of the complete list without frustrating players in their attempts to recall each item in the list. The total list should be read when the answer is given.

Demonstration.   This requires the player to perform a particular skill or task (Demonstrate how to "cut and paste" on the PC). This is one of the most engaging tests for adult learners.

● SETTING UP AND RUNNING A GAME

We now focus on the physical and mental preparation needed to set up and conduct a classroom game. This section deals with assembling the game accessories, pre-game set-up, game play, and closure.

Game Equipment

Game accessories are materials, equipment, or props that create an appropriate learning game environment. Here is a reminder list of some of the equipment, materials, and props used for the games in this book, along with hints on how they may be used during the game.

Flip Chart.   This standard of the training room can be used to reinforce key lecture points, display rules of play, or to hold an actual game board or chart for game play. One plus: Feedback comments, rules of play, and other posted charts can be taken down and stored for future use.

Computer + LCD Projector.   If your classroom is equipped with a computer set-up and an LCD projector, you can use a PowerPoint® presentation to display rules of play, question material, case studies, and other commentary. One plus: by using your laptop to adapt on-the-spot written material (instructions or feedback), you can create a valuable real-time game dynamic that adds to the quality of the experience.

Overhead Projector.   Overheads can be used to reinforce lecture points, display game format and rules of play, keep score, and list key elements of discussion or list comments and reactions—especially helpful for large groups. Use the overhead to display the rules of play, recreate the game sheet (Hard Case), present ongoing play (Virtual X-Change), or present the solution (Cash Box, Floor Plan, or Rear View Mirror).

Chalkboard.   Some team rooms are still equipped with the old-fashioned chalkboard. Like the flip chart,

> *Create your own game overview transparency.*
>
> Each game includes a "Player Instructions" sheet that can be easily replicated onto an overhead transparency and then displayed as the "rules of play" at the beginning of the game.

this can be used to reinforce key lecture points, display "bulletin board" messages or rules of play, and hold game charts or other communications written on newsprint.

Bulletin Boards.   Use these to post rules of play, present "theme" posters, display in-play game sheets, or post ongoing puzzles or commentary.

White Dry-Erase Board.   An alternate to the chalkboard, it can also be used to hang posters or charts. Some facilitators may want to create a game board using the board, attaching sticky magnets to the back of item cards or other game props.

Cassette Tape/CD.   The audio player is used to provide audio commentary, stories, or background music and to signal the beginning or end to each round of play.

Game Materials and Accessories

Masking Tape.   This indispensable item can be used to secure charts and posters on walls, post item cards onto wall charts, mend paper items, secure electrical wires to the floor or wall, and so on. For "floor games" (Floor Plan, Floor Teams, Rear View Mirror), masking tape is used to mark off the playing areas and establish "toe lines" for tossing objects at a target (Champions). Several catalog houses, such as Trainer's Warehouse (sales@trainerswarehouse.com), sell "flip chart border" masking tapes that have a continuing pattern that is not only attractive, but helpful in measuring and laying out the floor grids.

Felt-Tipped Markers.   These are the instruments that record information on flip charts and white boards. They can also be used to create or embellish game accessories, such as identification calling cards (Friendly Persuasion), passports (Passport), and team icons (Smack Down).

Posters or Charts.   Commercial posters or personally developed charts can be used to reinforce the learning and to create a playful game environment. "Theme" charts can underscore concepts from the curriculum, current events, or behavioral expectations.

Noisemaker.   The natural energy of game play can drown out even the most vigorous voice. An alternate noise can add to the playful game environment as well as save your voice. The noise serves as a way to alert players when to start or stop, acknowledge a correct response, signal that it's time to return from break, and so on. Some commonly found noisemakers include call bells (think "bell service" at a hotel), chimes, dinner bells, whistles, train whistles, and kazoos.

Timer.   This is a stopwatch, kitchen timer, or wristwatch with a second hand and is especially useful in timed sequences, such as rounds of play or a timed question-and-answer period.

Special Cards and Paper Sheets.

- *Large index cards* (5 x 8) create the identification cards used in Floor Plan and Floor Teams and the calling cards used in Friendly Persuasion. These cards can also be used as impromptu "voting" cards to indicate team feedback to a presentation or procedure (Second Mouse Gets the Cheese).

- *Name cards* are used to create team identities or team "icons" in Smack Down. You can make these cards by folding 5 by 8-inch cover stock in half.

- *Small index cards* (3 x 5) are used as ballots (Counter Intelligence), player identification cards (Proxy), or item cards (Ghostwriter and Having a Bad Hair Day).

- *Paper sheets.*
  - Ordinary sized paper sheets are used as game sheets for many of the games (photocopy, as needed), the "passport" used in Passport, as well as the special instruction sheets in Cash Box.
  - Small paper sheets are used for "virtual" communications in Virtual X-Change.

Game Markers.   Some games require a marker to temporarily cover a space or to indicate status on a game sheet.

- *Space markers.* Pawns or poker chips can be used to designate spaces for Floor Plan or Floor Teams. Other designations, such as simply marking an "X," can be used for Dragon Squares and Counter Intelligence.

- *Colored dots.* Adhesive dots, in blue, green, red, and yellow, are used in the "gathering" experiences of Friendly Persuasion and Passport.

- *Coins.* Batches of U.S. coins—ranging from 37 to 78 cents per set—are used to develop the "prototypes" in Cash Box. The real-time feel and play of actual monies helps in this specific game experience.

Game Cards.   Several games require game "cards," ranging from actual playing cards (Team Poker), to item cards used in Ghostwriter and Having a Bad Hair Day to the "proxy" cards used in Proxy.

Prize Tickets.   These are used for drawing prizes during or after game play. Tickets can be created using portions of 3 by 5-inch index cards or "raffle tickets" purchased in rolls from teacher supply catalogs and stores. (Some trainers like to award one ticket to EVERY player at the beginning of the session and then add one ticket from winning players. This gives everyone a chance to win the prize, with the winners receiving a slight edge.)

Containers.   Depending on the requirements of the game, containers can range from egg cartons (Cash Box) to dinnerware bowls and plates (Champions). Bowls can also be used to hold raffle tickets.

Game Set-Up

The "Golden Hour," the hour prior to conducting your game experience, is the critical time for readying the classroom and yourself—especially for the first play of the game. Take this time to mentally and physically revisit your audience and to check the intended play area as you walk through your game. Conduct an inspection of the training room; check for any hazards to safety or obstacles that could inhibit play and make sure your A/V equipment is in working order. Set up or move tables and chairs as required. Place posters, banners, worksheets, or wall charts containing suitable quotations or artwork as required.

After you feel satisfied with the safety and logistics of the room, take on the perspective of your students as you enter the room. Is the room visually attractive; does it set the stage for an active learning experience?

Instructor's Table.   Set aside one table or area as YOUR resource area. Take time to organize this table/area with the game sheets and accessories for easy access during game play.

- Lay out overhead transparencies, lecture notes, and additional reference materials (dictionary, reference manuals, or handouts), as required.

- Lay out game sheets and score sheets for distribution before and during the games.

- Lay out accessories such as noisemakers, masking tape, cards, and prizes, as necessary.

Preliminaries: Establishing the Environment

These are the in-class procedures prior to actual game play that help create the structure to the game and a "game play" environment. They include such steps, as required:

- Dividing the class into subgroups or teams.

- Seating each team at its own table.

- Lining up players in established game-play areas.

- Having teams select team names.

- Assigning roles to players, including procedures team members will use to respond to questions.

- Distributing game materials, including game sheets and paper and pencils.

- Distributing score sheets, question or problem sheets, and other game accessories and props.

- Displaying game information and player instructions.

- Introducing the rules of play, which is described in more detail below.

- Having teams fill out and submit their ballots, game sheets, or answer sheets.

Introducing the Rules of Play

The introduction is designed to engage the interest of participants. The introduction sets the stage for what is to follow and establishes both rules and expectations. The following is a sample introduction for the game Cash Box.

Sample Introduction: Cash Box

"Good afternoon. I want to briefly go over the game Cash Box. The game objective is for your team to assemble a prototype 'Cash Box' within the assigned time of 22 minutes. You will be divided into teams, and each team will be given a kit of supplies, including: Player Instruction Sheets, 75 cents in coins, one egg carton, a set of Post-it Notes, and game sheets. Your team will then be given 22 minutes to assemble the Cash Box in accordance with the Player Instructions."

[Show transparency of "Player Instructions" on overhead projector].

"You are to submit a readied product when time is called.

Good luck!"

Game Play

Games are played as described in the next session, "30 Games to Boost Performance." Here is an example, drawing once again on Cash Box.

1. Divide the group into teams of six players each. Have each team select a "Product Manager" to lead them through the exercise.

2. Distribute one Cash Box kit to each Product Manager.

3. After each team receives its kit, inform them they have 22 minutes to construct their product, a prototype "cash box," and then submit their Final Product Sheets when completed.

4. Start play.

5. Stop play after 22 minutes.

6. Collect a Final Product Sheet from each team.

7. Post the time received on each team's Final Product Sheet.

8. Award 25 points for each team that correctly assembled the Cash Box.

Game Closure

In the afterglow of a game, refocus participant attention on the key performance goals of the exercise. Closure is a process of helping participants to reflect on their experiences and develop meaningful learning. It entails any or all of the following:

- Reviewing and sharing observations of the game and game play.

- Tying up loose ends of the game and clarifying any confusion about the rules.

- Venting, where participants let off steam about the rules or any other constraints they experienced.

- Linking the behaviors that surfaced during game play with "real life" as it shows up in the workplace.

- Relating what was learned from the game material and from game play to relevant performance goals and concepts.

- Discussing any new information or insights raised during the game.

- Congratulating the players for their participation and acknowledging their contributions.

● POST-GAME DEBRIEFING: HARVESTING LEARNING THROUGH FACILITATION

It's said that what we hear, we forget; what we see grabs our attention; and what we do, we remember (Confucius). The point of debriefing is to help people "do" as a means to expand, enhance, and reinforce their learning. By "doing" and then discussing an activity as opposed to reading about, hearing about, or passively watching an activity, we physically engage participants in the learning experience.

In the past decade there has been a revival of interest in using simulations, team exercises, and "live play" as part and parcel of adult learning. One reason for this renaissance is realization that learning is not exclusively or primarily a mental task. In a very literal sense, physical activities help us "embody" learning. Physical application of intellectual constructs and principles is what builds skill—not just mental contemplation or discussion of those constructs and principles. Time spent thinking about a subject may be important, but it will not create mastery.

Definition

Facilitation is a technique of introducing subject matter, ideas, concepts, and facts to people in ways that actively engage them in their own learning processes. It relies more on asking questions than it does on providing answers. It requires not only mastery of the subject matter in question (usually referred to as content) but an ability to structure experiences, activities, and interactions that enable others to learn about, recall, and apply their content knowledge. Facilitation is also a philosophy of teaching that assumes that learning has a kinetic aspect we can only bring into play by physical activity. When we involve our muscles in learning, we learn more deeply.

Styles of Facilitation

How you perceive your role as a trainer will most certainly influence your facilitation style. Just as there is great variety in how people prefer to learn, there is great variety in how people prefer to teach and how they facilitate activities in order to put across their teaching points.

- If you see your role as being "the one who provides all the answers," you are apt to be a more directive facilitator. Your focus in an activity is to drive home your teaching point regardless of any other issues that may arise. You may be more focused on people's ability to find the right answer than on their ability to understand the process by which an answer may be found.

- If you see your role in more Socratic terms (that is, your job is to ask people questions that prompt them to think about what they have learned), you may focus more on the issues, dynamics, and interactions that crop up around the content and not just on the content itself. This is a more indirect approach to learning but can be equally effective in reinforcing content.

- If you feel that rules are meant to be obeyed, you may be uncomfortable with processing the kind of learning that can occur when people give themselves permission to "step outside the box" in carrying out an activity. In our notes to facilitators, we have tried to anticipate the various ways that this might happen and suggest questions you might ask to gain value from these outbreaks of creativity.

- If you feel that rules are just a starting point for exploring the art of the possible, we have tried to explain the rationale behind the rules so that you can keep an activity in some sort of bounds and not lose focus on your ultimate objective.

Whatever your style, the success of your facilitation efforts can be enhanced by focusing on the following keys to effective learning.

● KEYS TO EFFECTIVE LEARNING

1. Help People Understand the WHY of the Activity

More adults object to the term "game" than they do to the actual play involved. Rather than become involved in a long drawn-out semantic argument over whether this is a game or a simulation, exercise, or whatever, we suggest you introduce an activity along these lines:

The following activity is called [name of activity] and the point of this exercise is [pick one of the following]:

- To help us learn about [· · · + content or task]

- To discover the dynamics involved in [· · · + content or task]

- To reinforce our understanding of [· · · + content or task]

- To explore how this [· · · + content or task] applies to [. . .] our daily work or interactions

- To remember the key concepts of [· · · + content or task]

- To apply [· · · + content or task] in order to [. . .]

Any of these general goals should suffice to explain WHY this activity is pertinent and appropriate.

To facilitate learning, you need to communicate clearly WHAT participants are going to be doing. You can be far more general about WHY they are going to be doing it. A large part of learning will come from how you facilitate discussion about the WHY's of an activity in the aftermath of play.

You will occasionally run across someone who point-blank refuses to "play games." Assign that person the task of being a process observer, scorekeeper, logistics manager, or some other support role. Once you begin facilitating discussions after the activity, he or she can chime in with observations along with the rest of the teams.

2. Help People Understand the WHAT of the Activity

To reduce confusion, as well as wasted time and effort, make sure you thoroughly understand the rules of play for each activity. The best way to do this is by enlisting people to play with you in a practice session where you yourself are a participant. As you practice the game play, note any questions that arise. If something baffles you, it is apt to baffle others when it comes time to play. Note any connections that occur to you (such as, "This is the same sort of dilemma we encounter when we try to get consensus in staff meetings"). Go ahead and ask the suggested processing questions of your practice players so that you can anticipate the types of responses you are apt to encounter. Ask your practice players whether they made any connections with situations they encounter in "the real world." If necessary, reword the instructions using your own terms to make sure that you understand and can communicate exactly what needs to take place at each step in the process. If you cannot confidently explain the rules, it is doubtful that others will be able to follow them.

When you are asked to interpret a rule and the rule is clear (for example, "Only one person may ask a question of the other team"), simply reiterate the rule. On the other hand, if there is no firm definition of one way or the other as to how the rule might be interpreted, let the group interpret it for themselves. For example, the rule in Hard Case might say: "If the team's response is the most appropriate, advance the team's icon three spaces on the game chart." The team asks you as the facilitator, "How do we determine 'most appropriate'?" The obvious choices are that the team leader decides, or majority rules, or by consensus. A good response would be, "You decide" or "How would you normally determine appropriateness?" Force the group to examine its own assumptions and patterns of behavior.

Any time a question arises about rules and their interpretation, it should lead you to later ask:

- What are the factors that influence how we interpret the "rules"?

- How do those factors influence us in our day-to-day work or team decisions?

- What rules to we choose to follow and which do we choose to ignore?

- Who makes the rules?

- Who has the final word in interpreting the rules?

- What accounts for the gap between the rules and our day-to-day reality?

- When is it important to play by the rules and when is it OK to skirt around them?

3. Help the Group Manage Complaints

When someone complains about any aspect of the game, the best response is to ask, "What would you like to do or change?" The point is to help people take responsibility for their experience and for how they choose to participate in their own learning. Avoid explaining or rationalizing why something has been done. Focus instead on what the participants did and why they did so. Help the group take ownership of their own learning and empower them to make the changes that they think will improve the experience.

4. Help the Group Come to Terms with Consequences

Despite the fact that adults typically tend to learn more from analyzing their failure to perform than they do from assessing the reasons for their success, groups may blame you (or another team) for their failure to complete an activity or their inability to win. Blame is a reflexive way to displace uncomfortable feelings of incompetence or guilt. Teams might claim the following:

- The other team cheated because they stepped outside the rules.

- The instructions were unclear; there was no way we could win.

- You didn't give us enough time to complete the activity.

- This has nothing to do with real life.

- We were doomed from the start because . . .

Challenging defensive behavior head-on is rarely helpful. It tends to degenerate into "Yes, you did" and "No, I didn't" kinds of arguments. A more productive way of dealing with blaming behavior is to go back and reexamine the choices available. Although we cannot choose the situations we encounter, we can always choose our response to those situations. Go back to whatever situation is central to the complaint and engage the group in brainstorming what options are available in these kinds of situations. For example it is usually possible (not necessarily desirable) to:

- Reframe the question.

- Negotiate for an extension.

- Seek clarification.

- Renegotiate the rules.

- Withdraw.

- Passively resist.

- Maliciously comply.

- Adapt the group process to fit the situation.

- Reexamine our assumptions.

- Lodge a complaint and seek new terms.

The key point is to reinforce that we empower ourselves when we realize that we can choose and then exercise that power of choice. We can choose to blame others or we can choose to empower ourselves to change a situation or change our response to that situation.

5. Help the Group Manage Disagreements

When teams bog down in disagreements over what to do, who needs to do what, or how to proceed, you can intervene to help get them back on track. Here are some suggestions:

- Elicit what the group is currently doing, thinking, or feeling. The group will not be able to move forward until there is shared understanding of where they are right now.

- Separate facts (which can be tested) from assumptions and interpretations (which may be tacit, invisible, and unexamined). Identify the assumptions that each person brings to the situation and the interpretation that he or she is applying.

- Continue to probe for WHY participants believe or think what they do. Press on beyond "Just because I do" or "This is how we have to do it." Dig underneath the behavior to surface the assumptions and logic that prompted the behavior. Point out that unexamined assumptions frequently can lead us into unproductive behavior because it is difficult to get everyone on the same page when we are all beginning from different assumptions.

- Agree on the learning that took place. Develop agreements on immediate next steps based on that learning. What new approach does the team want to try?

- Try the new approach and see what happens. Does it offer a realistic alternative to proceed?

6. Help the Team Explore Resistance

Resistance is a natural phenomenon to be understood, not a sign of rebellion to be eliminated. When teams seem to be resisting an instruction, a rule, or a process, first acknowledge that the team is struggling and then ask participants to share what makes this task difficult for them. The following questions offer a means to better understand resistance:

- The instructions say to do . . . , and yet your team chose to do . . . What was your reasoning?

- Which parts of the game seemed to present a roadblock or difficulty for your team? What did you do to get under, over, around, or through this difficulty?

- Sometimes it feels as if we have been asked to do the impossible. What knowledge or resources do you think you needed that you did not have?

• Was there some aspect of the game that ran afoul of the way you normally work in teams? What was that? What is the reality of how you usually work in teams?

● FINAL THOUGHTS

Incorporating performance games into your lesson plan offers the unique opportunity for matching the personality of the game and its ability to bring dimensions of energy and focus to the demands of your curriculum and audience. And something quite unique: no matter how many times you play the same game, even with the same material, audience reaction to the game experience differs. Each group of participants invariably has its own learning thresholds and perceptions of what is new and important. One of your rewards is to experience the joy of discovery along with each audience.

30 Games to Boost Performance

Best of the Wurst

● PURPOSE

   - To create a dialog about the role on values in the workplace.

   - To identify the specific values that matter most to people.

● GAME OBJECTIVE

   To develop a consensus on the "best" of the worst.

● PLAYERS

   Eight or more.

● TIME

   Twenty-five to forty minutes.

● SUPPLIES

   - Deck of ten to fifteen index cards for each group.

   - Pens/pencils.

   - Set of blank index cards.

- An overhead projector (if using transparencies) or a newsprint flip chart and felt-tipped markers.

- Masking tape (optional).

- Noisemaker (optional).

● PREPARATIONS

For each team, prepare a deck of ten to fifteen index cards describing a variety of "worst" workplace situations. Include blank cards so teams can create their own "worst" situations. Alternative: Prepare a worksheet with "worst" situations. (For sample "conditions," please see Sample Play and General Comments.)

● GAME PLAY

1. Divide group into teams of four to six players each.

2. Give each group a deck of index cards or a worksheet describing a variety of workplace characteristics.

3. Give each group 10 minutes to select and rank those characteristics that are most likely to undermine productivity, squash creativity, and totally demotivate the workforce. (See General Comments: Team Voting.)

4. Have groups present their lists and then explain their rankings.

5. Using one blank index card for each selection, have players vote for the three "best" of the "worst" conditions or characteristics. (See Customizing: Scoring for point scoring system.)

● POST-GAME DEBRIEFING

After each team shares its top ten list, ask:

- What is the impact of each condition? How does this degrade or impede performance?

- What specific values came up for your team? If this were the "worst," what would you say constitutes the "best"?

- Is this situation an accurate description of your organization? If so, what changes would you suggest?

Ask participants: "How did you arrive at your ranking?"

- Was it a case of majority rules (the most votes win)?

- Was it through consensus building (where you fully discuss what is acceptable to most of the group most of time)?

- Or did the loudest voice win (the group gives in to whoever is the loudest or most forceful person)?

- Or did you abdicate the choice to one or more individuals (let Mike or Susie or the Project Manager decide)?

- What are the pros and cons of the decision-making approach you chose?

- Is the way you arrived at your decision typical of the way that most choices are made in your organization? What is the good news about that? What is the bad news about that?

● GENERAL COMMENTS

- Best of the Wurst was suggested by the framegame, "structured sharing," as described by Dr. Thiagarajan in his book, *Design Your Own Games and Activities*. Thanks, Thiagi.

- This is a wonderful way to vent "ain't it awful" sentiments. As in "Dilbert" cartoons, we can all relate to some of the "wurst" aspects of working for the Nachtmare Wurst Company. The role of the facilitator is to turn attention from venting about the "worst" aspects of work to discussion of what "better" or "best" conditions would look like. The underlying issue is one of values—a subject we rarely discuss in the workplace. This is an exercise that can help employees talk seriously about the values that matter most to them and the characteristics that help create a meaningful workplace. The Best of the Wurst can be used to compare a variety of best-worst issues such as working conditions, new product launches, leadership traits, leaders, organizations (within own industry or outside), and so forth.

- *Team Voting.* Teams can use several different methods to select their top ten "worst" conditions or characteristics that are apt to demoralize workers, lower productivity, or simply get in the way of completing the work.

They may arrive at this decision through:

- Simple voting—the most votes "win," aka, majority rules.

- Consensus—the process of discussion that arrives at a result that most participants can live with.

- Domination—the loudest voice wins, or whoever can dominate the group gets their way.

- Abdication—the group abdicates their right of choice by vesting it in a smaller group or a designated individual.

- The process by which the groups arrive at their decisions can provoke as much useful discussion as the decisions themselves.

Samples of Wurst Conditions

- No discretion allowed in how you do your job.

- No flexibility in the work schedule.

- Revolving door management.

- No linkage between performance and rewards.

- There is rampant favoritism.

- Management is disengaged and uncaring.

- No opportunity to learn or grow on the job.

- No opportunity to build one's skills.

- No opportunity for career growth.

- No one ever says thank you.

- No one ever willingly shares knowledge with others.

- Each unit sees itself in competition with all the others.

- No tools or support to help people learn or perform their jobs.

- People are punished for taking initiative.

- Suggestions for improvements are routinely ignored.

- Bureaucracy, rather than logic, governs procedures.

- Employees are routinely kept in the dark concerning current status or future plans.

- Employees have no say in how work is managed.

- Form is revered more than substance.

- Creativity is actively discouraged.

- Assignments are made on a purely arbitrary basis.

- The rules change unpredictably from one day to the next.

● SAMPLE PLAY

1. The group is divided into two teams—Team A and Team B.

2. Each player receives paper and pencil.

3. The facilitator provides the following instructions:

   You work for the Nachtmare Wurst Company, a meatpacking plant specializing in "wurst"—a variety of sausage or ground frankfurters. Despite the poor economy, people are leaving in droves and management has finally grasped that they have to get a handle on what people care about in order to persuade them to stay. Management has selected you and your colleagues as workforce representatives in a survey of worker values as a last-ditch effort to try to save the company.

   You have been given a deck of index cards describing some of the conditions about which people have complained in the past. There may be other items that your group considers important that you want to add. Use the blank index cards to do so. Your job is to identify the top ten "worst" aspects of working at Nachtmare Wurst Company and to suggest what management should do to address these problems.

4. The facilitator instructs the teams they have 10 minutes to create a list of ten items.

5. After 10 minutes the facilitator has each team present its list.

6. Team A presents its worst ten items:

   - No job security.

   - Dangerous working conditions.

   - Poor health coverage.

- Financially unstable company.

- Bad management (supervision).

- Hot and miserable plant environment.

- Noisy working conditions.

- Poor or no sick leave plan.

- Poor vacation leave.

- No concern for workers.

7. Team B presents its worst ten items:

   - No flexibility in the work schedule.

   - Revolving door management.

   - No linkage between performance and rewards.

   - There is rampant favoritism.

   - Management is disengaged and uncaring.

   - No opportunity to learn or grow on the job.

   - No opportunity to build one's skills.

   - No opportunity for career growth.

   - No one ever says thank you.

   - No one ever willingly shares knowledge with others.

8. The facilitator posts both lists.

9. Players use index cards to select their "favorite" top three items.

10. Final list: The "Best of the Wurst":

    a. Dangerous working conditions.

    b. Bad supervision.

    c. No concern for workers.

11. Dialog begins as to what workplace conditions contribute to a good job and a satisfying career.

● CUSTOMIZING BEST OF THE WURST

Size of Group

- For small groups, play as one team. Compare the list against a list developed by the facilitator from previous sessions.

- For medium groups, eight to twelve, play as two teams.

- For larger groups, play as prescribed, but allow more time for presentations and ranking of the final three.

Time of Play

- Shorten or lengthen the time allowed for team meetings and presentations, as necessary.

Method of Play

- Have players create their own "best of the worst" lists from scratch, and then compare these lists against your own or previously developed lists.

- Have each participant write down one or more "worst case" working condition, each one on its own index card. Collect the index cards and create one working list for the entire group. Divide the group into teams and have each team develop a ranked list from the index card items.

- For larger groups, conduct a secret ballot in which teams vote only on other teams' lists.

- Conduct this exercise before a break and allow your participants to review the item lists at their own pace.

- Suggest to participants that they think about an item or two for the next day's program and then begin the next day with the compilation of items on the list.

- Conduct this exercise and then conduct a brainstorming session on the other side of the topic. For instance, have participants compile a list of unsafe conditions in the plant and then brainstorm ways to improve plant safety.

- Conduct this exercise and then conduct a brainstorming session on the most important issues which management should address in order to improve productivity and employee satisfaction.

- Have each team record its items on a newsprint chart and then post the charts. Encourage teams to review and even add to other teams' charts during breaks.

- Provide guidance about developing basic protocols to avoid petty annoyances in intact work teams.

- Additional Rounds of Play. If your group is taking the content to a higher level—such as developing recommendations on how to overcome or remove annoyances that exist at the level of the group/organizational culture (i.e., lessening organizational aversion to risk)—expand by the game by one or two additional rounds of play.

Scoring

- Award 1 point for each selection made by the players. Tally the votes and declare the selection that received the most points the winner.

- Alternate scoring system. Issue one red dot, one blue dot, and one yellow dot to each player. Have players use these dots to award "first choice" (red), "second choice" (blue), and "third choice" (yellow).

- Tally the points by multiplying all first choices by 5 points, all second choices by 3 points, and all third choices by 1 point. The team with the most total points wins.

- Award bonus points for the most convincing presentation.

Best of the Wurst

· ·

- **Form teams of four or more players each.**

- **Review the set of workplace condition cards or worksheet that you receive.**

- **Prepare a list of the "top 10" worst conditions.**

- **Present your list to the entire group.**

- **Each player selects the three "best" of the worst conditions.**

- **Teams are awarded points based on player selections.**

Cash Box

- PURPOSE

    - To demonstrate the various contributory roles people play in team problem solving.

    - To demonstrate the dynamics of self-directed teams.

    - To highlight the importance of team communications.

- GAME OBJECTIVE

    To place coins in the appropriate position within the allotted time.

- PLAYERS

    Six or more.

- TIME

    Forty-five to sixty minutes.

- SUPPLIES

    - One Cash Box kit per team, consisting of:

        - One compartmental container. Empty egg cartons are excellent cash box containers—they are inexpensive, easy to stack and store, and easy to load during game play.

- 75 cents in change: 3 dimes, 5 nickels, 20 pennies.

- One Post-it® Note pad (to designate "empty" bins). You may have to remind your teams to use the Post-it Notes to designate the "empty" container bins. Every successful product assembly involved teams immediately recognizing and designating the empty bins.

- One Product Manager's Instruction Sheet.

- One Product Manager's Worksheet.

- One set, Advisor Instruction Sheets (five sheets).

  Assembly Note: Each Advisor Instruction Sheet headline is followed by one to five dots. These dots, all but invisible to the players, are reminders to the facilitator of the differing instructions to each player—"Advisor One" shows one dot, "Advisor Two" shows two dots, and so forth. This "dot" notation system will assist you while photocopying, assembling, and distributing the handouts.

- One Final Product Sheet.

- Stopwatch and whistle (optional).

- One flip chart easel and felt-tipped markers. Create a flip chart showing the time elapsed and which teams have completed the project. This will increase the competitiveness of play and prompt a discussion of the impact that deadlines and time pressures have on team communications in the workplace. Refer back to the flip chart to compare the "fastest" completions to the "most accurate."

- An overhead projector (if using transparencies).

- Paper and pens/pencils.

- Noisemaker (optional).

● GAME PLAY

1. Divide the group into teams of six players each.

2. Have each team select a "Product Manager" to lead them through the exercise.

3. Distribute one Cash Box kit to each Product Manager.

4. After each team receives its kit, inform them they have 22 minutes to construct their product, a prototype "cash box," and then submit their Final Product Sheets when completed.

5. Start play.

6. Stop play after 22 minutes.

7. Collect a Final Product Sheet from each team.

8. Post the time received on each team's Final Product Sheet.

9. Award 25 points for each team that correctly assembled the Cash Box.

● POST-GAME DEBRIEFING

This is an ideal game to demonstrate the concepts of team coordination and communication. Teams will be able to complete their products in direct proportion to how effectively they are able to share their information and coordinate tasks. To get at these issues, you may want to ask:

- Who was the "real" leader? Was it the assigned Product Manager or one of the Advisors (team members)?

In attempting to solve any problem, there are predictable questions that teams must answer. These include:

- What do we know?
- What do we not know?
- What do we assume about this situation?
- What are our resources?
- What are our options?
- What are our constraints?
- Who's going to do what?

There are also key roles that someone must assume if the team is to succeed. (*Note to Facilitators:* It is helpful to write these down in advance on a flip chart.) Take a few minutes and discuss in your team which individuals played any of the following roles. Come up with at least one example of how this role contributed to your performance.

Questioner—Someone who asks questions of the group.

Idea Generator—Someone who suggests options or alternatives.

Scribe—Someone who captures what is said, suggested, or attempted so that the team can remember.

Builder—Someone who takes an option that has been offered and expands or improves on the idea so that the group can put it to use.

Recruiter—Someone who assigns roles or delegates tasks.

Devil's Advocate—Someone who challenges the status quo assumptions about what is right or necessary.

Quality Assurance—Someone who checks to see if the group is actually accomplishing its tasks or fulfilling expectations.

Historian—Someone who looks at what has happened and helps the team learn in order to improve its future performance.

- Which role was most influential?
- Were any of these roles formally assigned or did these folks spontaneously take them on?
- What was the impact if this role was missing or disregarded?
- In our particular culture, what characteristics does it take to be effective in each of these roles?
- Are some of these roles not valued in our organization? With what result?
- How would the scribe be of assistance in figuring out that not all instructions are the same?
- How did your team's performance today resemble or differ from what typically happens on the job?

● GENERAL COMMENTS

- The first *AHA!* of the exercise comes when each team realizes that the five instructions contain different—and vital—pieces of the puzzle. Failure to assemble the product usually stems from an untested assumption that the instructions are identical. The processing point to make is that one of the first acts any team should take is to compare notes and make sure that everyone has access to the same data about the task, their resources, their constraints, and the situation.

- Note that in day-to-day work, the tools and templates we use (or egg cartons and coins) are an important aspect of how we coordinate and communicate. They serve to make tangible the processes we follow in working together.

- Simulate real-world updates by using the flip chart as a bulletin board to issue "information updates" (clues) to teams when they become muddled or fail to realize that the five instruction sheets contain differing clues. When teams did not grasp the numbering system of the bins, one facilitator posted a "recall notice" that informed teams that some of the containers were numbered incorrectly—only left to right. The teams immediately reread their instructions and made in-play corrections that allowed them to meet their deadlines.

● CUSTOMIZING CASH BOX

Size of Group

- If the group is small—five to eight players—form one team. This is a very favorable observation position for the facilitator.

- The minimum number of players for game play is five, requiring players to administer and coordinate the entire project themselves—a working example of a self-directed team.

- A team of seven or more players can include additional roles such as:

  - Supply Manager, to receive and distribute all materials.

  - Recorder, to document all coin placements and prepare the Final Product Sheet.

- Larger size groups require additional scrutiny from the facilitator, but are a dramatic and expedient way to demonstrate team dynamics. If possible, use an assistant to help in the distribution and collection of materials, as well as in responding to questions from the teams during game play.

Time of Play

- For more highly skilled groups, increase the difficulty of the exercise by reducing the time allowed to complete the task.

- Allow additional time for larger groups to deal with general issues of distribution and communications.

Method of Play

- Modify the level of play to suit your group.

  Example 1: Simplify Play. For less skilled groups, simplify the task by decreasing the number of coins and instructions.

  - Decrease the amount of change to 39 cents—1 dime, 3 nickels, and 14 pennies.

  - Rewrite the clues to reflect the following adjustments:

    Bin #1 = Empty (remove the dime, nickel, and penny).

    Bin #3 = 2 pennies (remove one dime).

    Bin #4 = 1 nickel (remove one nickel).

    Bin #11 = 1 nickel (remove two pennies).

    Bin #12 = 3 pennies (remove three pennies).

  Example 2: Complicate Play. For more highly skilled groups, complicate the task by including a "bogus" instruction in Advisor One's instructions and then placing a correction in Advisor Five's instructions.

  Change: Add this clue to Advisor One's instructions: "Bin 1 has three coins totaling 15 cents."

  Change: Add the word "Correction" to Advisor Five's instructions: "*Correction:* Bin 1 has three coins for 16 cents."

- Introduce "practice sessions" that require teams to perform sample tasks required in the exercise, such as coin counting (product identification).

  Example: "Bin 8 has six coins totaling 15 cents; identify the number and type of coins" (six coins = 1 dime + 5 pennies = 15 cents).

Scoring

- For early submission of a correct Final Product Sheet, award 2 bonus points for each minute before the deadline.

- For incomplete or partially correct Final Product Sheets, award 2 points for each bin correctly assembled.

PLAYER INSTRUCTIONS FOR
Cash Box

- Form teams of six players:

   1 Product Manager who:

   Receives the raw materials.

   Oversees product assembly.

   Submits Final Product Sheet.

   5 Advisors, who assist in assembly.

- Your team receives a kit containing:

   1 Model 18B Cash Box container.

   Raw materials:

   3 dimes, 5 nickels, 20 pennies.

   1 Post-it® Note pad.

   1 Product Manager's Instruction Sheet.

   1 set, Advisor Instruction Sheets.

   1 Product Manager's Worksheet.

   1 Final Product Sheet.

- Your team has 22 minutes to submit
  a correct Final Product Sheet.

PRODUCT MANAGER'S INSTRUCTION SHEET FOR
Cash Box

• •

Your employer has a new product, the Model 18B Cash Box, a special placement of coins arranged in their own containers. Cash Box will provide hours of entertainment for children ages 8 to 13.

Your task is to coordinate the assembly of the product and then prepare the Final Product Sheet and submit it to the facilitator.

Your team has been given these materials to assemble the Model 18B Cash Box:

- One prototype container, standard issue with 12 bins.

- Twenty-eight coins amounting to 75 cents.

To help you with the assignment, you have been given the following instructions and worksheets:

- One Product Manager's Worksheet, to assist you in the recording and placement of coins into the appropriate bins. The worksheet allows you document all information on a bin-by-bin basis.

- One set of Advisor Instruction Sheets—one sheet for each of your five "Advisors."

- One set of Post-it Notes to assist you as needed.

- One Final Product Sheet to record your final product.

Your task is to distribute one Advisor Instruction Sheet to each of your advisors, coordinate the assembly of the product, and then prepare the Final Product Sheet for submission to the facilitator.

Good luck!

PRODUCT MANAGER'S WORKSHEET FOR
Cash Box

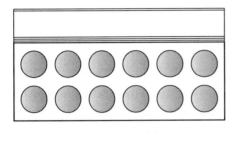

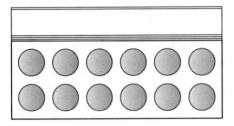

Bin 1_____

Bin 2_____

Bin 3_____

Bin 4_____

Bin 5_____

Bin 6_____

Bin 7_____

Bin 8_____

Bin 9_____

Bin 10_____

Bin 11_____

Bin 12_____

ADVISOR INSTRUCTION SHEET FOR
Cash Box.

• •

Your employer has a new product, the Model 18B Cash Box, a special placement of coins arranged in their own containers. Cash Box will provide hours of entertainment for children ages 8 to 13.

Your team has been given:

- One prototype container, standard issue with twelve bins.

- Twenty-eight coins amounting to 75 cents.

- Post-it Notes, sets of instructions, a worksheet, and a Final Product Sheet.

Your assignment is to select and place the appropriate arrangement of coins from the information provided. Additional information:

- The standard issue container is divided into two rows with pockets numbered 1 to 12.

- One upper-row empty bin is next to a pocket containing two coins.

- There are six coins each in bins 8 and 12.

ADVISOR INSTRUCTION SHEET FOR
Cash Box..

Your employer has a new product, the Model 18B Cash Box, a special placement of coins arranged in their own containers. Cash Box will provide hours of entertainment for children ages 8 to 13.

Your team has been given:

- One prototype container, standard issue with twelve bins.

- Twenty-eight coins amounting to 75 cents.

- Post-it Notes, sets of instructions, a worksheet, and a Final Product Sheet.

Your assignment is to select and place the appropriate arrangement of coins from the information provided. Additional information:

- Nine bins contain one or more coins.

- Bin 4 is the only bin with two coins.

- One of the outer bins on the bottom row contains six pennies.

- The bin with three pennies is above an empty bin.

ADVISOR INSTRUCTION SHEET FOR
Cash Box...

• •

Your employer has a new product, the Model 18B Cash Box, a special placement of coins arranged in their own containers. Cash Box will provide hours of entertainment for children, ages 8 to 13.

Your team has been given:

- One prototype container, standard issue with twelve bins.

- Twenty-eight coins amounting to 75 cents.

- Post-it Notes, sets of instructions, a worksheet, and a Final Product Sheet.

Your assignment is to select and place the appropriate arrangement of coins from the information provided. Additional information:

- Bin 8 has six coins totaling 15 cents.

- There are two empty bins in the top row.

- There are a total of three nickels positioned in two vertical bins.

- Bins 9 and 10 contain only one coin each, totaling 6 cents.

ADVISOR INSTRUCTION SHEET FOR
Cash Box....

• •

Your employer has a new product, the Model 18B Cash Box, a special placement of coins arranged in their own containers. Cash Box will provide hours of entertainment for children ages 8 to 13.

Your team has been given:

- One prototype container, standard issue with twelve bins.

- Twenty-eight coins amounting to 75 cents.

- Post-it Notes, sets of instructions, a worksheet, and a Final Product Sheet.

Your assignment is to select and place the appropriate arrangement of coins from the information provided. Additional information:

- Bin 9 contains one mid-value coin.

- The empty bin in the lower row is next to the bin containing 15 cents.

- Bin 11 contains 7 cents.

- There is an empty bin above the bin containing three coins.

ADVISOR INSTRUCTION SHEET FOR
Cash Box.....

Your employer has a new product, the Model 18B Cash Box, a special placement of coins arranged in their own containers. Cash Box will provide hours of entertainment for children ages 8 to 13.

Your team has been given:

- One prototype container, standard issue with twelve bins.

- Twenty-eight coins amounting to 75 cents.

- Post-it Notes, sets of instructions, a worksheet, and a Final Product Sheet.

Your assignment is to select and place the appropriate arrangement of coins from the information provided. Additional information:

- Standard container upper bins are numbered 1 to 6, left to right.

- Standard container lower bins are numbered 12 to 7, left to right.

- The bin over the bin with one penny has three coins totaling 12 cents.

- Bin 1 contains three coins for 16 cents.

FINAL PRODUCT SHEET FOR
Cash Box

TEAM # _____

TIME _____

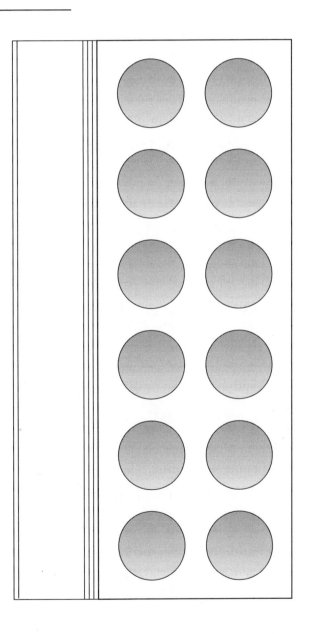

Cash Box

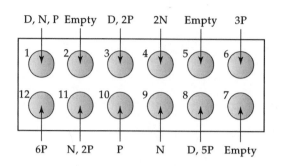

Advisor #1:   Container is divided into two rows, with pockets numbered 1 to 12.

Upper-row empty bin is next to pocket containing two coins.

There are six coins each in bins 8 and 12.

Advisor #2:   Nine bins contain one or more coins.

Bin 4 is the only bin with two coins.

One of the outer bins on the bottom row contains six pennies.

The bin with three pennies is above an empty bin.

Advisor #3:   Bin 8 has six coins totaling 15 cents.

Two empty bins in the top row.

Total of three nickels positioned in two vertical bins.

Bins 9 and 10 contain only one coin each, totaling 6 cents.

Advisor #4:   Bin 9 contains one mid-value coin.

Empty bin in the lower row is next to the bin containing 15 cents.

Bin 11 contains 7 cents.

Empty bin is above the bin containing three coins.

Advisor #5:   Upper bins are numbered 1 to 6, left to right.

Lower bins are numbered 12 to 7, left to right.

Bin over the bin with one penny has three coins, totaling 12 cents.

Bin 1 contains three coins for 16 cents.

Champions

● PURPOSE

- To demonstrate how well the participants understand the topic.

- To create a dynamic learning environment.

- To emphasize the importance of playing to individual team member strengths.

● GAME OBJECTIVE

To score the most team points.

● PLAYERS

Nine to twenty-four.

● TIME

Thirty to sixty minutes.

● SUPPLIES

- One Question Sheet per team for each round of play.

- One target (a 10-inch dinner plate with a 4-inch bowl in center).

- One set of three soft throwing objects (bean bag, Koosh™ ball).

- A newsprint flip chart and felt-tipped markers to post the ongoing scores.

- An overhead projector (if using transparencies).

- Masking tape to designate "toe lines" for the target throw.

- One noisemaker (optional).

● PREPARATION

Create a score sheet on a flip chart or chalkboard to record ongoing scores and number of earned target throws.

Create a target by placing a 4-inch bowl on top of an ordinary 10-inch dinner plate.

Place the target in the center of a conference or instructor's table.

Using masking tape, set-up a "toe line," a line behind which players throw objects at the target. The toe line should be 6 to 7 feet from the target to discourage players from leaning over and dropping the balls onto the target.

● GAME PLAY

1. Divide group into three teams—A, B, and C.

2. Each team selects two "knowledge" champions and one "throw" champion.

   - The "knowledge" champions try to earn up to three throws at the target by correctly responding to the Question Sheets.

   - The "throw" champion attempts to convert the earned throws into team points by throwing objects at the target.

3. Designate Team A as the "home team."

Round 1: Question Time

1. Distribute Question Sheet #1 to each team.

2. Have knowledge champions write their team designator on the Question Sheet.

3. Give players 3 minutes to respond to questions.

---

4. Call time after 3 minutes.

5. Have Team A, the "home team," select their three best question responses—the three responses they feel are the most correct.

6. Post the three question numbers on the flip chart or chalkboard.

7. Remind all teams that responses to these three questions selected by Team A will be the ONLY responses that earn throws at the target.

8. Collect one Question Sheet from each set of "knowledge" champions.

9. Go over Question Sheet #1.

10. Award one throw at the target for each correct response to one of the "three best" questions.

11. Indicate how many throws each team earned.

Round 1: Target Throw

1. Each team sends its "throw" champion to the target to convert the earned throws into points.

Each throw earns points, as follows:

- In the center bowl = 5 points.

- On the target or plate = 2 points.

- Off the plate or target = 0 points.

2. Tally and record the score for each team.

This concludes the first round of play.

Round 2

1. Designate Team B as "home" team.

2. Distribute Question Sheet #2.

3. Have Team B designate their "three best responses."

4. Award target throws based on the accuracy of the responses to Team B's "three best."

5. Target throws are the same as in Round 1.

Round 3

1. Designate Team C as the "home team."

2. Distribute Question Sheet #3.

3. Have Team C designate their "three best responses."

4. Award target throws based on the accuracy of the responses to Team C's "three best."

5. Target throws are the same as in Round 1 and Round 2.

End of Game

The team with the most points is declared the winner.

POST-GAME DEBRIEFING

After the conclusion of the game, ask the teams:

- What was your basis for selecting your three best responses?

- How did you pick your knowledge champions? What expectations did you have of them and how did you communicate those expectations?

- How did you pick your throw champion? What expectations did you have of them and how did you communicate those expectations?

- How can we better communicate our individual strengths to our teammates so that they can consciously play to those strengths?

- *Knowledge Champions:* What did you expect in the way of support from your teammates?

- *Throw Champions:* What did you expect in the way of support from your teammates?

- What, if any, coaching took place between rounds of play?

- What coaching or performance feedback would have been useful?

- How does coaching or performance feedback improve our confidence?

- What sort of feedback or coaching do we usually get in the workplace?

- What are your lessons learned from Champions that will boost your team performance?

At play, at work, and in life we know we are doing well because we receive feedback to that effect. If we are never specifically praised for what we do or how we do it, we assume we are doing OK, but have no way of knowing how we might improve. In the absence of regular, focused, and specific feedback we are stuck doing things as we've always done them.

● GENERAL COMMENTS

- At first glance, this game may seem a little complicated, but the proof is in the play. For the past three semesters students at UMBC selected Champions as the favorite review game because of the quality of its play—a competitive game environment that encourages both mental AND physical skills within the group.

- *Home Field Advantage.* A unique feature of Champions is the creation of a rotating "home field advantage." Allowing each team, in turn, to determine that the "target throw" selections are based on matching THEIR best three responses simulates this "advantage." So it comes as no surprise that "home" teams earned a whopping 50 percent more tosses during their rounds than their opponents did.

- Remind teams that they may change their knowledge and throwing champions between rounds. This reminds teams of ongoing issues of delegation and personnel selection.

- Champions provides an opportunity to not only reinforce job or task specific knowledge, but to demonstrate the value of coaching, both in developing our substantive knowledge and in our ability to physically carry out assigned tasks.

- Use soft throwing objects such as Koosh balls or beanbags; they work much better than tennis or Ping-Pong balls, which tend to bounce off the target.

- Allow teams to keep their own scores. This simplifies your administrative duties. If there is any question about self-scoring cheating, this can lead to an interesting discussion of workplace ethics and "doing anything" to win.

- Allow throwers one or two practice tosses before their first turn. You may also allow each team a two-minute audition to select a throwing champion.

- Once played, the ball stays where it lands. If thrower makes a bulls-eye (ball in center or in bowl), leave the ball in the bulls-eye for the rest of the thrower's turn.

● SAMPLE PLAY

1. The group of fifteen participants is divided into three teams of five players each—Team A, Team B, and Team C.

2. Each team selects two "knowledge" champions and a "throw" champion.

3. Team A is designated as the "home team."

Round 1: Team A Is "Home Team"

Question Time

- Facilitator distributes Question Sheet #1: Sales Management.

- Each team's knowledge champion responds to Question Sheet #1.

- Facilitator calls time after 3 minutes.

- Team A selects its three top responses—questions 1, 3, and 5.

- Facilitator collects Question Sheet #1 from each set of "knowledge" champions.

- Facilitator goes over the question set, but only awards a throw for each correct response to questions 1, 3, and 5.

Scoring

- Team A responded correctly to questions 1, 3, and 5.

Team A earns three target throws.

- Team B responded correctly to question 5; their responses to questions 1 and 3 were incorrect.

Team B earns one target throw.

- Team C responded correctly to questions 1 and 5; their response to question 3 was incorrect.

Team C earns two target throws.

Target Time

Team A: Three Throws

- Team A's thrower "champion" placed the first two throws onto the plate; the third throw landed off the plate.

Team A receives 2 points for each throw onto the plate, for a total of 4 points.

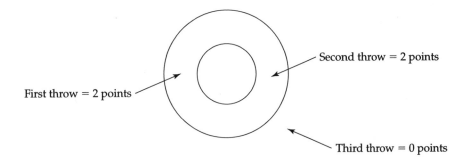

Team B: One Throw

- Team B's thrower "champion" placed her only throw onto the plate.

Team B receives 2 points.

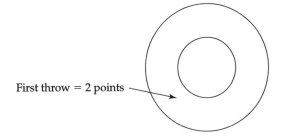

Team C: Two Throws

- Team C's thrower "champion" placed one throw into the center bowl; the second throw landed off of the plate.

Team B receives 5 points for the center bowl throw.

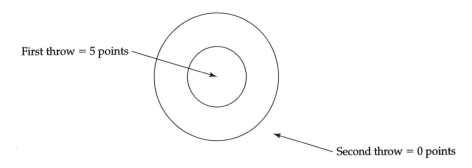

Scoring: Round 1

> Team A = 4 points
>
> Team B = 2 points
>
> Team C = 5 points

Round 2: Team B Is "Home Team"

- Facilitator distributes Question Sheet #2: Stress Management.

- Facilitator calls time after 3 minutes.

- Team B selects its top three responses—questions 1, 2, and 4.

- Facilitator goes over the question set, but only awards a target throw for each correct response to questions 1, 2, and 4.

- Play is the same as for Round 1.

Round 3: Team C Is "Home Team"

- Facilitator distributes Question Sheet #3: Time Management.

- Facilitator calls time after 3 minutes.

- Team C selects its top three responses—questions 3, 4, and 5.

- Facilitator goes over the question set, but only awards a target throw for each correct response to questions 3, 4, and 5.

- Play is the same as for Rounds 1 and 2.

End of Game

- The facilitator tallies the points from the three rounds of play.

- The team with the most points wins.

● CUSTOMIZING CHAMPIONS

Size of Group

- For smaller groups of six to ten players, divide group into two teams.

- For medium-sized groups of fifteen to twenty-four, divide into three teams. Encourage each team to share the roles of knowledge and throw champion among all players.

- For larger-sized groups of over 25:

  - Prepare additional question sheets and divide into four to seven teams. Because of the additional players, recruit one or two assistants to help distribute and then collect the game sheets and keep track of the scoring.

  - Play separate rounds with one set of teams while other teams observe—the TV-game show format provides entertaining viewing and all players can learn from the topic questions discussed.

Time of Play

- Shorten or lengthen the time for a round of play depending on the difficulty of the topic or size of the group.

Method of Play

- Create a level playing field by allowing all teams to select their three best responses. Post the question numbers on the score sheet and then award target throws as appropriate.

- Distribute one Question Sheet to each player. At the end of the round have each team select one player's Question Sheet to represent the team. This could lead to an interesting discussion on how each team selected its representative Question Sheet.

- To introduce more familiarity into the question material, create a mix of questions on well-known generic topics as well as on your topic.

- Use organizational topics such as personnel, production, marketing, accounting, and plant safety.

- Use a short case study and ask a series of questions about the study.

- Increase the question set to seven (keeping the three "best"); reduce the question set to four (keeping the three "best").

Scoring

- Award a 3-point bonus to any team who correctly responds to all five questions.

PLAYER INSTRUCTIONS FOR
Champions

••

- **Form 3 teams—A, B, and C.**
- **Select three champions from your team—two knowledge, one thrower.**

Round 1: Team A Is Home Team

- **Take 3 minutes to complete Question Sheets.**
- **Team A selects its three best responses.**
- **For all teams, one throw is awarded for each correct response to the questions chosen by Team A.**
- **Thrower champions take their earned throws.**

Scoring

- **Each throw in Bull's Eye = 5 points.**
- **Each throw into target area = 2 points.**
- **Each throw NOT in target area = 0 points.**

Subsequent Rounds

- **All rounds are played the same, but the home team rotates.**
- **The team with the most points wins.**

QUESTION SHEET #1: SALES MANAGEMENT FOR
Champions

● ●

1. What Chicago merchant coined the phrase "the customer is always right"?

2. Telephone sales calls made to clients with whom you have no previous relationship of any kind are called _____ _____.

3. A customer in a retail store seems nervous and refuses to make eye contact. The best sales tactic is to (a) not interrupt or interfere or (b) offer assistance.

4. Name the type of marketing that sends information about the product or service directly to the prospect.

5. When using a direct mail strategy, which is the better incentive—cash discounts or premiums?

QUESTION SHEET #2: STRESS MANAGEMENT FOR
Champions

••

1. Rest is the only thing that restores the wear and tear on our body. True or False?

2. What beverage is the most frequently consumed source of caffeine in the United States?

3. Because of their high cholesterol, eggs cannot be used as a source of protein. True or False?

4. What is the most powerful stressor—anxiety, loss of control, or frustration?

5. What is the most effective type of exercise for trimming body fat—aerobic, toe touches, or power lifting?

QUESTION SHEET #3: TIME MANAGEMENT FOR
Champions

•••

1. What is the number one time waster—telephone interruptions, drop-in visitors, or crisis management?

2. Name the most critical feature of ANY filing or storage system.

3. Who are more likely to make and then follow a daily "to-do" list—men or women?

4. According to secretaries THIS is their most frequently performed activity.

5. A clear desk actually improves your ability to manage time more effectively. True or False?

FACILITATOR'S ANSWER SHEET FOR
Champions

• •

Sheet #1

1. Marshall Field. (Try to give customers what they want without arguing.)

2. Cold calls.

3. (b) Offer assistance. (Nervous customers are frequently shoplifters.)

4. Direct mail (mail order).

5. Premiums (token gifts, coupons, gift with purchase).

Sheet #2

1. True. (Proper diet gives you energy, but rest rejuvenates you.)

2. Coffee.

3. False. (Egg whites are an excellent source of protein.)

4. Loss of control.

5. Aerobics. (Toe touches are good for flexibility; power lifting for strengthening.)

Sheet #3

1. Crisis management.

2. Information retrieval—finding what you are looking for.

3. Women (Priority Management Study).

4. Answering the telephone.

5. True (fewer distractions).

Clue Less

• •

● PURPOSE

- To promote critical thinking and problem-solving skills in teams.

● GAME OBJECTIVE

To solve the scenarios in the shortest possible time.

● PLAYERS

Six or more.

● TIME

Fifteen to thirty minutes per round.

● SUPPLIES

- Four or more problems, each containing a set of clues, prepared in advance by the facilitator. (See Sample Game Play section and Additional Scenario Sheet for examples.)

- One Time Card for each team.

- One Master Time Card to track team scoring.

- An overhead projector (if using transparencies) or a newsprint flip chart and felt-tipped markers for tracking ongoing time cards.

- Masking tape.

- Paper and pencils for each team.

- Noisemaker (optional).

● GAME PLAY

1. Divide the group into teams of four to six players each.

2. Have each team sit at its own table.

3. Distribute one Time Card to each team.

Round 1

1. Introduce the first scenario/problem.

2. Present the first clue.

3. Give each team 3 minutes to try to solve the case problem and charge the team 1 hour for the clue.

4. Have each team write down its response on its Time Card.

5. Review each team's response.

   - If the response is correct, this completes the team's round.

   - If the response is incorrect, team continues to play.

6. Present clues until all teams have solved the problem or all clues have been given. All teams are charged 1 hour for each clue it requires to solve the problem.

7. Post the hours charged for each team.

Subsequent Rounds

Play is the same for each round, with a different problem/scenario being presented for each round.

End of Game

1. Tally all the team scores.

2. The team that solved the scenario using the least number of hours wins.

● POST-GAME DEBRIEFING

When a team brainstorms, it is as important to understand the process that led to the decision as the decision itself. The following questions prompt teams to think about their thought processes and the impact that these processes had on their success or failure.

- What assumptions do you think your team made about the limits on possible solutions?

- Did you dismiss any solutions as "too off the wall"?

- Did you set up any kind of process for selecting an answer or did you just allow anyone who thought that he or she had an answer to submit it on behalf of the team?

- Did your team set up any sort of a process for capturing what you knew? If so, what was the value of writing down ideas and facts?

Successful teams are usually a combination of sensors (people who focus on the facts) and intuitors (people who focus on the possibilities). You can help teams understand the dynamics of these two groups through the following questions:

- Who on your team took the facts and tried to lay them out in some sort of logical order? What was the value of doing that?

- Who on your team began brainstorming different interpretations or possible solutions? What was the value of doing that?

- If you could hand pick a team, who would you rather have, more of the fact folks, more of the possibility people, or some balance of the two? Why is that?

● GENERAL COMMENTS

- Although, strictly speaking, the brain is not a muscle, it does benefit from exercise. Clue Less is designed to help teams exercise their mental muscles by actively testing their assumptions as part of the problem-solving process.

Prompt players to ask broad questions within their teams about the range of things that might be happening in a situation.

- Encourage players to be logical, imaginative, straightforward, and devious all at the same time. Instruct them that when one line of reasoning runs into a brick wall, they should reexamine their assumptions and start again.

- Clue Less requires both a deductive reasoning mentality and an ability to reason laterally. The group will be given one clue at a time and each team can take a guess after every clue—just like solving a mystery. This paradoxical process is called lateral thinking—the ability to develop imaginative solutions to existing problems.

- We suggest you use this recipe as a "starter" for composing your own mystery. Start by focusing on one teaching point. Develop a set of facts that provide details to the teaching point or lead one to a specific conclusion concerning why someone acted as he or she did. Arrange these facts in a specific order. Decide the order you want to establish for your clues and then arrange the clues:

  - From the most difficult to the most simple (or the other way around).

  - From the earliest dates or times to the most recent dates or times.

  - From data based on who, what, where, when, and why to how.

● SAMPLE PLAY

Preparations

1. Select an important scenario you wish discussed within your group.

2. Create a mini-case study to introduce the scenario and set the tone for the series of clues that lead to the solution or conclusion of the scenario.

3. Develop a set of five to six facts that lead to the solution.

4. Rewrite each fact into a clue.

5. Sequence the clues into an order to present the information, such as the most difficult clue (first) to the easiest clue (last).

Game Play

1. Divide the group into four teams of four to six players each.

2. Have each team meet at its own table.

3. Distribute one Time Card, paper, and pencils to each team.

4. Have each team enter its name on their Time Card.

5. Introduce the scenario: This is the story of a man who forgot his five-digit house number. Our job is to help him find his house number with the fewest number of clues. The five-digit house number is composed of four single-digit numbers—specifically 0, 1, 2, 3—with one of the single-digit numbers used twice.

Clue 1

- The first clue is read aloud: "The five-digit number ends with a score."

- Teams record their responses on the first clue of the Time Card.

- No team presents the correct solution.

- Charge Teams A, B, C, and D 1 hour.

- (All teams interpreted "score" as 20 and placed a "two" and "zero" in the last two digits.)

- ☐ ☐ ☐ 2 0

Clue 2

- The second clue is read aloud: "The five-digit number starts with the lowest primary number."

- Teams record their responses on the second clue of the Time Card.

- No team presents the correct solution.

- Charge Teams A, B, C, and D 1 hour.

- (All teams interpreted "lowest primary number" as "one" and placed it in the first digit.)

- 1 ☐ ☐ 2 0

Clue 3

- The third clue is read aloud: "The middle single-digit number is the sum of all other numbers."

- Teams record their responses on the third clue of the Time Card.

- Team C identifies the solution. This concludes its round.

- Teams A, B, and D are still working on the case.

- Charge Teams A, B, C, and D 1 hour.

- (All teams interpreted "sum" as 1 + 0 + 2" and placed "three" in the middle or third digit. Team C inferred that if the middle digit was "three," the missing number was "zero" and placed that in the second digit.)

- $\boxed{1}$ $\boxed{}$ $\boxed{3}$ $\boxed{2}$ $\boxed{0}$

Clue 4

- The fourth clue is read aloud: "The value of the last two digits is double the value of the first two digits."

- Teams record their responses on the fourth clue of the Time Card.

- Teams A, B, and D identify the solution. This concludes their round.

- Charge Teams A, B, and D 1 hour.

(Teams A, B, and D determined that the last two digits, "20," were twice the value of the first two digits, "10," and placed a "zero" in the second digit.)

- $\boxed{1}$ $\boxed{0}$ $\boxed{3}$ $\boxed{2}$ $\boxed{0}$

Scoring

1. The facilitator posts the Master Time Card.

Time Charged

| | Clue # → | | | | |
	I	II	III	IV	Total Hours
Team A	1	1	1	1	4
Team B	1	1	1	1	4
Team C	1	1	1	0	3
Team D	1	1	1	1	4

Subsequent Rounds

Play is the same for each round.

End of Game

The team with the lowest number of hours wins.

● CUSTOMIZING CLUE LESS

Size of Group

- Have smaller groups—from six to ten—play as two teams.

- For larger groups, divide the group into teams of five.

Time

- Shorten or lengthen the problem-solving time depending on the difficulty of the clue, the case, or the level of the audience.

Method of Play

- *Lightning Round.* Create a lightning round case study. Present each clue, give teams 20 seconds to respond, and then move on to the next clue. The first team to solve the scenario wins.

- *Question-and-Answer.* Allow each team to submit one question in writing per round. Charge the question-writing team 1 hour per question.

- *Elimination Rounds.* Establish a "par" or standard number of clues. Present clues and field responses. Any team that cannot solve the scenario/problem by par is eliminated from future rounds.

- *One-on-One.* Conduct a lightning round with one team at a time. Present each clue and allow 20 seconds for the team's oral response. Continue until the team solves the scenario or you exhaust your clues.

Scoring

- Award bonus "times" for teams that solve the case in the fewest clues. The bonus times are hours that are deducted from the total score.

PLAYER INSTRUCTIONS FOR
Clue Less

- Form two or more teams.

First Clue

- After the scenario has been introduced, receive the first clue.

  - *Scoring:* If your response is . . .

    - *Correct,* this ends your turn. Your team is charged 1 hour.

    - *Incorrect,* continue play. Your team is charged 1 hour.

Subsequent Clues

- All clues are received and responded to in the same fashion.

End of Game

- The team with the lowest number of charged hours wins.

TIME CARD FOR
Clue Less

• •

Scenario # _____   Team _____

Clue 1: _____

Solution: _____

Correct? _____   Time Charged _____

- -

Clue 2: _____

Solution: _____

Correct? _____   Time Charged _____

- -

Clue 3: _____

Solution: _____

Correct? _____   Time Charged _____

- -

Clue 4: _____

Solution: _____

Correct? _____   Time Charged _____

- -

Clue 5: _____

Solution: _____

Correct? _____   Time Charged _____

- -

Clue 6: _____

Solution: _____

Correct? _____   Time Charged _____

Total Time Charged _____

MASTER TIME CARD FOR
Clue Less

Scenario One: Time Card

	Clue 1	Clue 2	Clue 3	Clue 4	Clue 5	Clue 6	Total Hours
Team A							
Team B							
Team C							
Team D							
Team E							

Scenario Two: Time Card

	Clue 1	Clue 2	Clue 3	Clue 4	Clue 5	Clue 6	Total Hours
Team A							
Team B							
Team C							
Team D							
Team E							

MASTER TIME CARD FOR
Clue Less

· ·

Scenario Three: Time Card

	Clue 1	Clue 2	Clue 3	Clue 4	Clue 5	Clue 6	Total Hours
Team A							
Team B							
Team C							
Team D							
Team E							

Final Tally

	Sc. #1	Sc. #2	Sc. #3	Total Hours
Team A				
Team B				
Team C				
Team D				
Team E				

ADDITIONAL SCENARIO FOR
Clue Less

•••

New Product Introduction: Porcelain

Scenario: This product is found in every household. The product is made from a mix of kaolin (pure white clay) and petuntse (found in granite). The kaolin and pentuntse are fired (baked) at temperatures of 2280° F or 1250° C. At the high firing temperature the petuntse melts together to form a nonporous, nature glass and fuses with the kaolin to hold its shape.

Clue 1: The sturdiest example of this product is a ceramic product used for electrical insulators and laboratory equipment.

Clue 2: There are three types of this product—(1) hard-paste (circa 7th century), (2) soft-paste (circa 16th century), and (3) bone china (circa 18th century).

Clue 3: This ceramic product, often called "china" or "chinaware," because it was first made in China, is highly prized for its beauty and strength.

Clue 4: This product is known primarily as a material for high-quality vases and tableware, as well as for figurines.

Clue 5: Contemporary products of the soft-paste include English Wedgwood, Japanese Noritake, German Rosenthal, and American Lenox.

Counter Intelligence

....

● **PURPOSE**

- To explore the effect of a competitive environment.

- To demonstrate planning and strategy in a pressure situation.

● **GAME OBJECTIVE**

The first team to score 21 points wins.

● **PLAYERS**

Six or more.

● **TIME**

Twenty to fifty-five minutes.

● **SUPPLIES**

- One Game Sheet for each set of teams.

- One set of index cards per set of teams.

- An overhead projector (if using transparencies) or a newsprint flip chart and felt-tipped markers for posting scores.

- Paper and pencils for each team.

- Timer and noisemaker (optional).

● GAME PLAY

1. Divide into sets of two teams—Team X and Team O.

2. Have each set of teams sit at its own table.

3. Distribute one Game Sheet and several index cards to each set of two teams.

Team X is the playing team for the first round.

Round 1

1. The playing team, Team X, secretly selects a space on the Game Sheet and marks the space number on its index card.

2. After Team X selects its space, the opposing team (Team O) gets to ask a question of Team X before selecting its own space.

Sample Question Format: Is your mark in an inside square? In an outside square? In an even-numbered square? In an odd-numbered square? In a corner square?

3. Team O then selects a space and writes the space number on its index card.

4. If the spaces selected by the playing AND the opposing team . . .

- *Do NOT match:* The playing team marks the space with its symbol.

- *Match:* Both teams mark the space with their symbol.

5. This completes the turn.

6. Teams tally their scores (see Scoring below).

7. Play alternates to the opposing team (Team O).

Subsequent Rounds

Play is the same for all rounds.

Scoring

1. Each team tallies the number of spaces bearing its mark.

2. Each team receives:

- 1 point for each space bearing their team's mark.

- 5 points for covering three spaces in a row (a "3-set").

- 10 points for covering four spaces in a row (a "4-set").

3. The first team to score 21 or more points wins.

● POST-GAME DEBRIEFING

Even in situations where our goal is to collaborate (rather than compete) it's difficult to do so unless we:

- Understand how the other side defines success.

- Identify the assumptions they are making about the situation.

- Understand their plan or strategy.

- Get a handle on how they are thinking about us.

Counter Intelligence is, at its most basic level, a game about knowledge and strategy. The following questions will help participants focus on the elements that give rise to team strategy:

- Based on the information you were given, what options did your team identify for making your marks?

- Did you identify any particular constraints on how you placed your marks?

- What did you believe you knew about the other team?

- What constraints did you think they faced?

- Who on your team took the initiative to either offer or write down different strategies?

- How would you describe the strategy you selected and used? What were the strengths and weaknesses of that strategy?

- What did you learn about the value of having a strategy from this experience?

Counter Intelligence is also a game about information. Game play gives participants practice in refining and improving their ability to ask questions so that they can better understand, and therefore predict, the actions of other players. Because both teams can get credit for a well-placed mark, there is an incentive in this game both to be truthful and to collaborate with others. While there is no guarantee that even a well-worded and hard-to-evade question will produce a truthful response, the process of asking questions and evaluating answers brings up several important points for teams. These include:

- What incentives or disincentives are there to collaborate with others in this game?

- How do we seek to understand those who appear to be our opponents?

- How do we go about understanding how other people think?

- How can we identify the assumptions that others make about a situation?

- How can we ask questions in ways that give us more (rather than fewer) useful answers?

- How do you learn about how to ask productive questions?

- What led you to answer truthfully or deceptively when the other team asked you questions?

- What were the consequences of your answers?

- How can we increase the probability that the questions we ask will be answered truthfully?

- What can we offer in exchange when we ask others to be honest?

● GENERAL COMMENTS

- Before game play, remind your players that when an opposing (non-playing) team correctly identifies the space selected by the playing team, BOTH teams equally share that space, thus neutralizing any advantage the playing team gains from this round. This also points to the need to develop and follow a strategy, rather than merely responding to what the other teams do.

- Counter Intelligence can be won by clever strategizing—such as "bunching your spaces" in the center, allowing you to build "three-sets" and even "four-sets." This is the strategy used by Team X in Sample Play.

● SAMPLE PLAY

1. Group is divided into one set of two teams—Team X and Team O.

2. The Game Sheet and index cards are distributed to the teams.

Round 1

1. The playing team, Team X, selects and marks space 6 on its index card.

2. Team O inquires: "Did you mark an even-numbered space?"

3. Team X responds: "Yes."

4. Team O selects space 10 and marks it on its index card.

5. The two teams show their cards—the spaces do NOT match.

6. Team X marks space 6 with an "X."

1	2	3	4
5	6	7	8
9	10	11	12
13	14	15	16

7. This completes play for Round 1.

   Team X = 1 point.

8. Play alternates to Team O.

Round 2

1. Team O selects "space 11" and marks this on its index card.

2. Team X inquires: "Did you mark an odd-numbered space?"

3. Team O responds: "Yes."

4. Team X selects space 7.

5. The two teams show their index cards—the spaces do NOT match.

6. Team O marks space 11 with an "O."

1	2	3	4
5	6 ×	7	8
9	10	11 O	12
13	14	15	16

7. This completes play for Round 2.

   Score: Team X = 1 point; Team O = 1 point.

8. Play alternates to Team X.

Round 3

1. Team X marks "space 10" on its index card.

2. Team O inquires: "Did you mark an inside space?"

3. Team X responds: "Yes."

4. Team O selects space 10.

5. The two teams show their cards—the spaces MATCH.

6. BOTH teams mark space 10.

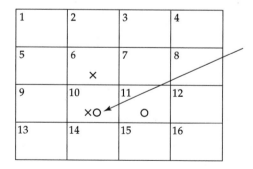

1	2	3	4
5	6 ×	7	8
9	10 ×O	11 O	12
13	14	15	16

7. This completes play for Round 3.

   Score: Team X = 2 points; Team O = 2 points.

8. Play alternates to Team O.

Round 4

1. Team O marks "space 12" on its index card.

2. Team X inquires: "Did you mark an inside space?"

3. Team O hesitates, then responds: "No."

4. Team X selects space 9.

5. The two teams show their cards—the spaces do NOT match.

6. Team O marks space 12 with an "O."

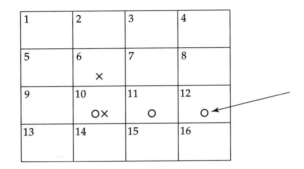

7. This completes play for Round 4.

   Score: Team O = 8 points (three covered and one "three-set");
   Team X = 2 points.

8. Play alternates to Team X.

Round 5

1. Team X marks "space 9" on its index card.

2. Team O inquires: "Did you mark an inside space?"

3. Team X responds: "No."

4. Team O selects space 14.

5. The two teams show their cards—the spaces do NOT match.

6. Team X marks space 9 with an "X."

1	2	3	4
5	6 ✕	7	8
9 ✕	10 O✕	11 O	12 O
13	14	15	16

7. This completes play for Round 5.

Score: Team O = 8 points; Team X = 3 points.

8. Play alternates to Team O.

Round 6

1. Team O marks "space 7" on its index card.

2. Team X inquires: "Did you mark an inside space?"

3. Team O responds: "Yes."

4. Team X selects space 7.

5. The two teams show their cards—the spaces MATCH.

6. Both teams mark space 7.

1	2	3	4
5	6 ✕	7 O✕	8
9 ✕	10 O✕	11 O	12 O
13	14	15	16

7. This completes play for Round 6.

Score: Team O = 9 points; Team X = 4 points.

8. Play alternates to Team X.

Round 7

1. Team X marks "space 13" on its index card.

2. Team O inquires: "Did you mark an inside space?"

3. Team X responds: "No."

4. Team O selects space 4 and marks it on their index card.

5. The two teams show their cards—the spaces do NOT match.

6. Team X marks space 13 with an "X."

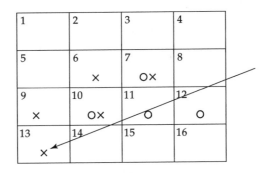

7. This completes play for Round 7.

   Score: Team X = 10 points (five covered spaces + one "three-set");
            Team O = 9 points.

8. Play alternates to Team O.

Round 8

1. Team O marks "space 15" on its index card.

2. Team X inquires: "Did you mark an inside space?"

3. Team O responds: "No."

4. Team X selects space 3 and marks it on their index card.

5. The two teams show their cards—the spaces do NOT match.

6. Team O marks space 15 with an "O."

1	2	3	4
5	6 ✕	7 O✕	8
9 ✕	10 O✕	11 O	12 O
13 ✕	14	15 O	16

7. This completes play for Round 8.

Score: Team O = 15 points (five covered and two "three-sets");
Team X = 10 points.

8. Play alternates to Team X.

Round 9

1. Team X marks "space 5" on its index card.

2. Team O inquires: "Did you mark an outside space?"

3. Team X responds: "Yes."

4. Team O selects space 4.

5. The two teams show their cards—the spaces do NOT match.

6. Team X marks space 5 with an "X."

1	2	3	4
5 ✕	6 ✕	7 O✕	8
9 ✕	10 O✕	11 O	12 O
13 ✕	14	15 O	16

7. This completes play for Round 9.

8. Team X scores 21 points to win.

Final Scoring

- Team X = 21 points

  [6 points (1 point for each covered space: 5, 6, 7, 9, 10, 13) + 15 points
  (5 points for three "three-sets": 5, 6, 7 + 5, 9, 13 + 7, 10, 13)]

- Team O = 15 points

  [5 points (1 point for spaces 7, 10, 11, 12, and 15) + 10 points
  (5 points for two "three-sets": 10, 11, 12 + 7, 11, 15)]

● CUSTOMIZING COUNTER INTELLIGENCE

Size of Group

- For groups of six to ten, play as one set of two teams.

- For larger groups, divide into sets of two teams and play all games simultaneously. Be sure to allow more time for game play of a larger group.

Time of Play

- Shorten or lengthen the time of play, especially for the first round, until players become familiar with the game play.

Method of Play

- *Alternate rule.* Have opposing team make their inquiry AFTER they plan their move. Does this "after the fact" data collection have any relevance or value?

- *Alternate rule.* Give pre-game instructions to each set of teams. Instruct one team to give incorrect feedback to their opponents. In the debriefing, ask the teams what happens when one side of an equation is inconsistent. Does that lead to inconsistencies and reprisals on both sides?

Scoring

- Shorten play by awarding 2 points for each space covered, 7 points for each "three-set," and 15 points for each "four-set."

PLAYER INSTRUCTIONS FOR
Counter Intelligence

....

- Divide into sets of two teams.

- Team X secretly selects an open space on the Game Sheet.

- Team O questions Team X about the placement of the space.

- Team O selects the space it believes was selected by the playing team.

- If the moves . . .

  Do NOT Match: Team X marks the space on the Game Sheet.

  Match: BOTH Teams—X and O—mark the space on the Game Sheet.

- Play continues until a team scores 21 points.

Counter Intelligence

1	2	3	4
5	6	7	8
9	10	11	12
13	14	15	16

Double Play

•••

● **PURPOSE**

- To prompt teams to think through the process of change.

- To reenergize a group with a quick brainstorming activity.

- To demonstrate critical thinking skills used in problem solving.

● **GAME OBJECTIVE**

To score the most team points.

● **PLAYERS**

Nine to thirty.

● **TIME**

Thirty to sixty minutes.

● **SUPPLIES**

- Five worksheets and pencils or pens for each team.

- An overhead projector (if using transparencies) or newsprint and felt-tipped markers for posting word pairs and solutions.

- Stopwatch or timing device.

- Noisemaker (optional).

● PREPARATION

Select five word pairs (see Double Play Sample Word Changes list for examples).

Write each pair of words on one Worksheet.

Prepare enough sets of the five Worksheets so that each team will receive a set.

● GAME PLAY

1. Divide the group into teams of three to five players.

2. Distribute one set of Worksheets to each team.

3. Explain that teams will have 7 minutes to transform, in a series of word changes—one letter for each word change—as many pairs of words as possible.

Rules of the Word Change

- Each acceptable word change costs the team "one change."

- Only one letter may be changed at a time, as follows:

  Changing one letter in place (bale to balk).

  Drop one letter, add one letter (foil to file).

  Anagram—rearrange word order (silo to soil).

- All words must have the same number of letters.

- All words must be found in a desktop dictionary.

- Present an example:

  Change WORD-to-WISE = WORD-wore-wire-WISE

4. Begin play.

5. Call time after 7 minutes.

6. Collect one set of Worksheets from each team.

Scoring

1. Award 5 points for each pair of words transformed.

2. Award a 3-point bonus for the team that used the fewest words to transform the word pair.

3. Declare the team with the most points the winner.

● POST-GAME DEBRIEFING

Here are some suggested questions that may help the players think through their experience in the activity:

- What was the hardest part of getting started? How did you approach the process of substitution and change?

- Who had the first breakthrough? How easy or difficult was it for them to get the team's attention?

- Did your performance improve in successive rounds? What became easier?

- Who played what role in helping the teams move forward?

- Who found this a very easy process? Did they make an attempt to explain their process to the team? Did this make a difference?

- Who found this a very difficult process? What was the impact on the team?

- Who was tempted to solve it by yourself rather than work collaboratively? What impact did this have on the team?

- Did any other factors slow you down? If so, what?

- What impact did a sense of competition have on your ability to solve the word transformation?

- How did the process you used in your team shift over time?

If you use this game to facilitate a discussion of what it takes for groups to embrace change, select from the following questions:

- What is an example of a recent "change initiative" that the group has experienced?

- What was the sequence of events that led up to this change?

- What was the sequence of events that took place within the change itself?

- What were the "moving pieces" affected in this change?

- What were the relationships that were affected by the change?

- What did those who were leading this change forget to address?

- How long did it take to bring about the change?

- How could the process have been shortened or made less painful?

If you use this game to facilitate a discussion of what it takes for teams to succeed, ask:

- What impact does clear success criteria have on team performance?

  (It enables teams to "keep score" and get immediate feedback on how well they are doing.)

- What happens when there are clear incentives that link performance to rewards?

- How do criteria help you see who is, or is not, contributing?

- What would it be like in the workplace if we had clear criteria for determining the "best way to skin a cat" and were left to our own discretion and imagination to reach that goal?

To link the experience of game play back to the workplace and to normal team behaviors, consider the following questions:

- What are the challenges in working out a method for doing work in your real life team?

- What is the first step in figuring out who will do what?

- What is your preferred way to contribute to team efforts?

- What are examples of "what has worked" and "what hasn't worked" when you tried to use your preferred approach?

- When a team is challenged to turn one thing into something else, what are the common barriers?

- What is the impact of knowing the ultimate goal (what the transformation needs to look like when you are done)?

- How often do you know in advance what the ultimate goal is?

- How do you establish a method or process when the ultimate goal is unclear?

● GENERAL COMMENTS

- This game was suggested by a word exercise developed by the mathematician and author, Charles Dodgson, also known as Lewis Carroll, author of *Alice in Wonderland*.

- Rarely are there any "silver bullets" that bring about immediate, painless change in an organization. We like to think that change is as simple as starting one thing or stopping another, but, as in Double Play, we usually find that there are any number of relationships or combinations that are affected. In any complex system (one with five or more people in it), effective change involves a number of moving parts. As in Double Play, change is not just a matter of moving around or altering individual elements of the situation. It also requires attention to sequencing, relationships, and rules (rules of spelling in this case).

- Remember the cliché "There's more than one way to skin a cat"? There are lots of ways to accomplish most tasks, but rarely are there strong, consistent, coherent explanations or incentives for skinning a cat in one particular way. Much of the impetus behind efforts to develop a "Balanced Scorecard" for federal agencies, departments, and offices is based on the notion that we need solid, well-understood criteria for measuring success if we are, in fact, determined to succeed. In Double Play clear criteria are established for measuring the best way to skin a cat—namely to do it in the fewest possible steps. For example, the Sample Play example shows moving from FOUR to FIVE in six steps. This can also be done in three steps: FOUR – foul – foil – file – FIVE.

● SAMPLE PLAY

1. Divide the group into two teams—Team A and Team B.

2. Give each team a set of Worksheets.

3. Post five pairs of words:

   FOUR to FIVE

   HEAD to TAIL

   NOSE to CHIN

   RIDE to WALK

   SINK to SWIM

4. Ask each team to write each pair of words on a separate Worksheet.

5. Give teams 7 minutes to transform as many pairs of words as possible.

6. After 7 minutes call time and collect the Worksheets from each team.

Sample Worksheets Submitted

Both teams solved three of the five pairs of words.

Team A's Solutions

FOUR – pour – poor – pool – fool – foot – fort – fore – fire – FIVE (8)

HEAD – heal – teal – tell – tall – TAIL (4)

SINK – sine – sane – sand – send – sent – seat – swat – swam – SWIM (8)

RIDE – side – silk – salk – WALK

Team B's Solutions

FOUR – fore – fire – FIVE (2)

RIDE – bide – bade – bale – balk – WALK (4)

SINK – skin – skim – SWIM (2)

Scoring

- Team A = 18 points

    FOUR to FIVE in eight word changes = 5 points

    HEAD to TAIL in four word changes = 5 points + 3 point bonus*

    SINK to SWIM in eight word changes = 5 points

    RIDE to WALK, disqualified, two errors:

        SIDE to SILK—two letters were changed

        SILK to SALK—"salk" not found in dictionary

- Team B = 24 points

    FOUR to FIVE in two word changes = 5 points + 3 point bonus*

    RIDE to WALK in four word changes = 5 points + 3 point bonus*

    SINK to SWIM in two word changes = 5 points + 3 point bonus*

*Bonus for using fewest words to complete transformation.

● CUSTOMIZING DOUBLE PLAY

Size of Group

- For smaller groups of six to ten players, divide group into two teams.
- For larger sized groups:
  - Play separate rounds with one set of teams while the other teams observe the play and debriefing.
  - Prepare enough Worksheets and then conduct as a whole group game. Take additional time to process and debrief the game.

Time of Play

- Shorten or lengthen the time for a round of play, depending on the difficulty of the word pairs or size of the group.

Method of Play

- Post sheets with additional word pairs on the wall to encourage random play during breaks.
- Allow teams to share information to reinforce cooperative learning.
- Allow teams to use references such as dictionaries. This demonstrates how learning aids or technologies add to solution capability of the team.
- Allow only one team to use references, such as dictionaries. This will introduce topics of ethics in team play or the competitive approach of "winning at all costs."
- Encourage individual play at puzzles for the fun of it and as a vocabulary-building exercise. Establish a "par" or standard number of word changes allowed per each pair of words as a guide for individual puzzle solving.
- Assign puzzles as a take-home exercise for completion at a later time.
- Debrief in terms of who sought other players' input and problem-solving techniques.

Scoring

- Award 25 points for each solution but subtract 2 points for each word used in the transformation.

Double Play

- **Form teams of three to five players.**

- **Receive five Worksheets, one for each word pair.**

- **Take 7 minutes to complete as many word transformations as possible.**

- **Turn in Worksheets after 7 minutes.**

- **Scoring: Your team receives . . .**

    5 points for each acceptable solution.

    0 points for any unacceptable solutions.

    3-point bonus for each transformation with the fewest changes.

- **The team with the most points wins.**

WORKSHEET FOR
Double Play

• •

How to Use This Worksheet

For the pair of words shown below, enter each one-letter change, according to the rules provided by the facilitator, to go from Word 1 to Word 2. Some examples are provided:

Examples: Boy to Man   Lose to Find

                Bay   Lone

                Ban   Line

                Man   Fine

                                   Find

Word #1   Word #2

Double Play

Here are some sample words with suggested solutions that you can reference or use in your own games. Remember, these are just examples of one way to solve the puzzles.

BOY to MAN—bay → ban

DEAD to LIFE—deal → lead → lied

DOG to CAT—cog → cot

EAST to WEST—fast → fest

FAIR to FOUL—fail → foil

FALL to RISE—fill → file → rile

FOUR to FIVE—fore → fire

GOLD to BOND—told → bold

GOOD to FAIL—gold → told → toll → tall → tail

HAND to FOOT—band → bond → fond → food

HEAD to TAIL—heal → teal → tell → tall

HELP to MOVE—held → meld → mold → mole

HOME to WORK—some → sore → wore

HOUR to YEAR—sour → soar → sear

LINE to BALL—lane → land → band → bald

JUNK to BOND—dunk → dune → done → bone

LADY to LASS—lads

LAST to LEAD—lost → loot → loan → load

LION to LAMB—line → lime → lame

LOSE to FIND—lone → line → fine

MEET to SAFE—melt → malt → male → sale

MESS to TIDY—less → lest → list → tilt → tile → tide

MOOT to REAL—molt → melt → meat → meal

NAY to YES—say → sat → set → yet

NOSE to CHIN—pose → post → cost → coot → coop → chop → chip

OLD to NEW—odd → add → aid → fid → fed → few

PINK to BLUE—sink → silk → slit → slut → slue

PLAY to GAME—plat → flat → fate → fame

RIDE to WALK—bide → bade → bale → balk

ROCK to BAND—rack → rake → rank → bank

SICK to WELL—silk → sill → sell

SINK to SWIM—skin → skim

STOP to MOVE—post → pose → pore → more

Dragon Squares

● ●

● **PURPOSE**

- To demonstrate the dynamics of collaboration versus competition.

● **GAME OBJECTIVE**

To score the most points.

● **PLAYERS**

Four or more.

● **TIME**

Fifteen to forty-five minutes.

● **SUPPLIES**

- One Game Sheet for each team.

- Paper and pencils for players.

- An overhead projector (if using transparencies) or a newsprint flip chart and felt-tipped markers for posting scores and comments.

- Noisemaker (optional).

● GAME PLAY

1. Divide the group into sets of two teams, one to three players on a team:

   - One team, "Dragons"

   - One team, "Hunters"

2. Distribute one Game Sheet to each team.

Round 1

1. Dragons select two squares on their Game Sheet.

2. At the same time, the Hunters try to identify both squares selected by the Dragons on the Hunter's Game Sheet.

Scoring

If the Hunters identify:

- *Both squares:* Hunters receive 3 points, Dragons receive none.

- *One square:* both Hunters and Dragons receive 1 point each.

- *Neither square:* Dragons receive 3 points, Hunters receive none.

Subsequent Rounds

All rounds are played in the same fashion.

End of Game

1. End game play after four or more rounds.

2. The team(s) with the most points win(s).

● POST-GAME DEBRIEFING

This is a simple collaboration exercise with profound implications for how we think about knowledge and the benefits of collaboration. The challenge is in seeing how long it takes teams to understand this, and then to do it effectively.

After Round 2, ask:

Hunters

- "What is your strategy for amassing the most points?"

- "If you keep on with your current strategy, what is the maximum number of points you are likely to score in the next three rounds?"

Dragons

- "What is your strategy for amassing the most points?"

- "If you keep on with your current strategy, what is the maximum number of points you are likely to score in the next three rounds?"

Both Teams

- "What do you assume about the relationship between Hunters and Dragons?"

- "If you were to alter your assumptions about the necessary relationship between Hunters and Dragons are there any other strategies you might want to explore?"

After Round 4, ask:

Hunters

- "How are you doing with your strategy? Is it working?"

Dragons

- "How are you doing with your strategy? Is it working?"

If there has been no change in team behavior, you may want to note that there is nothing in the rules that prohibits the Hunters from opening up a dialog with the Dragons. Offer a 10-minute "truce" for both sides to explore the art of the possible.

After any round in which two or more teams of Hunters and Dragons decide to swap information so that they can jointly maximize the number of points they earn, call a halt to the play and start to process the learning about collaboration. The following questions can get the discussion under way:

- When any situation appears to be a "zero sum game" where one side advances only at the cost of the other side, we are more apt to think about competition than collaboration. What led you to decide that this was a competitive situation?

- How did your team go about developing its strategy?

- What assumptions did you discuss?

- What led you to consider the possibility of collaboration between Hunters and Dragons?

- What shifts needed to take place before you could act on the possibility of collaboration?

- What makes it hard to collaborate in the workplace?

- In what situation is it easier to collaborate in the workplace?

- When we think about "winning" do we more typically assume a competitive situation or a collaborative situation?

- Who took the lead in helping you think through how your team might win in a collaborative situation?

- What sorts of behaviors are needed in order to make a collaborative relationship succeed?

● GENERAL COMMENTS

- This game was suggested by the ancient tale about a Dragon who guards a pearl of great treasure (in Asian mythology this great treasure is usually assumed to be knowledge and wisdom rather than material or physical wealth). To succeed in sharing the wealth (assuming that knowledge is an infinitely divisible good rather than a finite resource that must be jealously hoarded), both Hunters and Dragons must figure out how to collaborate—something they never seem to do in the storybooks.

- On the surface this game appears to be a simple, competitive guessing game. Can the Hunters guess where the Dragon is and can the Dragon successfully hide? The game objective, "To score the most points" does not, however, specify that either the Hunters or Dragons need to compete to rack up points against each other. They can, quite legitimately, decide to collaboratively score the maximum number of points in the time available. The question is: "What does it take for either team to stumble on this option and then to decide to pursue this strategy?"

● SAMPLE PLAY

    1. The group is divided into one set of teams—Dragons and Hunters.

    2. Each team receives a Game Sheet.

Round 1

    1. The Dragons select two squares, as indicated:

    2. The Hunters select two squares, as indicated:

    3. Both the Hunters and the Dragons have selected one square in common (the upper-left square).

    4. Both Hunters and Dragons receive 1 point each.

    5. This completes Round 1. Score = Dragons 1; Hunters 1.

Round 2

    1. The Dragons select two squares, as indicated:

    2. The Hunters select two squares, as indicated:

    3. The Dragons and the Hunters have selected the same squares.

    4. The Hunters receive 3 points; the Dragons receive 0 points.

    5. This completes Round 2. Score = Hunters 4; Dragons 1.

Round 3

    1. The Dragons select two squares, as indicated:

    2. The Hunters select two squares, as indicated:

    3. The Dragons and the Hunters have selected different sets of squares.

---

4. The Hunters receive 0 points; the Dragons receive 3 points.

5. This completes Round 3. Score = Dragons 4; Hunters 4.

Round 4

1. The Dragons select two squares, as indicated:

2. The Hunters select two squares, as indicated:

3. The Dragons and the Hunters have selected different squares.

4. The Dragons receive 3 points; the Hunters receive 0 points.

5. This completes Round 4. Score = Dragons 7; Hunters 4.

End of Game

1. The facilitator chooses to end the game.

2. The Dragons win.

● CUSTOMIZING DRAGON SQUARES

Size of Group

- For small groups, divide into one set of two teams.

- For groups numbering twenty or more, conduct several games simultaneously.

Time of Play

- Lengthen play by expanding the number of rounds to ten.

- Play for a specific number of rounds or a set time period.

Method of Play

- Introduce "intelligence reports" to the Hunters, indicating where one of the Dragons' squares is located. (Dragon teams are instructed to place an X in that square.)

- Interrupt game play to discuss team scores. If the teams indicate they wish to collaborate, suggest a 2-minute meeting between teams and then resume play.

Scoring

- Introduce an alternate scoring system awarding 10 points for acquiring both squares as opposed to 3 points each for getting one square each. Does this revised scoring lead to greater collaboration?

PLAYER INSTRUCTIONS FOR

Dragon Squares

....

- Form sets of two teams—Dragons and Hunters.

- Dragons select two squares on their Game Sheet.

- Hunters select two squares on their Game Sheet.

- Scoring is based on the number of squares chosen by the Dragons that the Hunters correctly identify.

- If the Hunters correctly identify:

  Both Squares: Hunters receive 3 points; Dragons receive 0 points.

  One Square: Hunters receive 1 point; Dragons receive 1 point.

  Neither Square: Hunters receive 0 points; Dragons receive 3 points.

- All rounds are played in the same fashion.

- The team with the most points wins.

Dragon Squares

			Dragon	Hunters
☐	Round 1	☐ Both squares ☐ One square ☐ No squares	Score _____	_____
☐	Round 2	☐ Both squares ☐ One square ☐ No squares	Score _____	_____
☐	Round 3	☐ Both squares ☐ One square ☐ No squares	Score _____	_____
☐	Round 4	☐ Both squares ☐ One square ☐ No squares	Score _____	_____
☐	Round 5	☐ Both squares ☐ One square ☐ No squares	Score _____	_____
☐	Round 6	☐ Both squares ☐ One square ☐ No squares	Score _____	_____
☐	Round 7	☐ Both squares ☐ One square ☐ No squares	Score _____	_____
☐	Round 8	☐ Both squares ☐ One square ☐ No squares	Score _____	_____
☐	Round 9	☐ Both squares ☐ One square ☐ No squares	Score _____	_____
☐	Round 10	☐ Both squares ☐ One square ☐ No squares	Score _____	_____

Floor Plan

● ●

● **PURPOSE**

- To explore the elements of effective team planning.

- To demonstrate the different roles in planning, coaching, and execution that team members play in establishing and executing a plan.

● **GAME OBJECTIVE**

To win by making the appropriate changes within the shortest amount of time.

● **PLAYERS**

Eight or more.

● **TIME**

Thirty-five to fifty-five minutes.

● **SUPPLIES**

- One roll of masking tape.

- Overhead projector (if using transparencies).

- One set of six 5-inch × 8-inch index cards for each Floor Team.

- One set of nine blank 5-inch × 8-inch index cards for each Floor Manager.

- One set of six markers—three red, three white—for each Planner (use red and white chips, checkers, buttons, or even dice).

- One Starting/Ending Design Sheet.

- One Directions Sheet for each Planner.

- One set of Instruction Sheets for each team:

  One Planner Instruction Sheet.

  One Floor Manager Instruction Sheet.

  One Floor Team Instruction Sheet.

- Noisemaker (optional).

- One stopwatch per operating Floor Team.

● PREPARATION

Create a floor "playing grid" (three-by-three Tic-Tac-Toe grid) as follows:

- Using masking tape, outline a six-foot square on the floor.

- Divide this square into two-foot sections, creating a three-by-three grid.

Using six of the 5-inch × 8-inch index cards, create a set of three "X" and three "O" cards for each Floor Team by marking them on both sides for easier identification.

Create the Starting/Ending Design Sheet. Use the Solution Sheets for examples or create your own design. The Design Sheet should only contain the starting and ending patterns, not the solution.

● GAME PLAY

1. Divide the group into sets of one or more teams, eight players to a team.

2. Distribute a set of "X" and "O" markers to each team.

3. Have each team select:

  One Planner

  One Floor Manager

  Six Floor Team members

4. Distribute the Instruction Sheets and other supplies to the Planner, Floor Manager, and Floor Team.

Planning Round: 5 Minutes

1. Give the Planner his or her Instruction Sheet, Starting/Ending Design Sheet, Directions Sheet, and six planning markers. The Planner should:

   - Develop a step-by-step plan to complete the floor maneuver in the fewest possible moves.

   - Record the step-by-step plan onto the Directions Sheet.

2. At the end of the 5 minutes the Planner:

   - Gives the Directions Sheet to the Floor Manager.

   - Meets with his or her Floor Manager to discuss execution of the maneuver.

3. The Floor Manager is given an Instruction Sheet, a set of three "X" and three "O" cards, and nine blank index cards. While the Planner is developing the plan, the Floor Manager should:

   - Prepare the floor grid for the maneuver.

   - Meet with his or her Floor Team to practice floor moves on the floor grid.

   - Meet with the Planner to discuss execution of the maneuver.

4. At the end of the 5 minutes the Floor Manager:

   - Meets with his or her Planner to discuss execution of the maneuver.

   - Receives the set of Directions Sheets from the Planner.

5. The Floor Team is given a copy of the Floor Team Instruction Sheet, three "X" cards, and three "O" cards. The Floor Team should:

   - Assist the Floor Manager in preparing the grid, as required.

   - Review the rules of the move.

   - Assign the three "X" and three "O" cards to specific players.

   - Practice floor moves with the Floor Manager.

Meeting Round: 2 minutes

The Planner meets with the Floor Manager to discuss the Directions Sheet.

Floor Maneuver: 3 minutes

The Floor Manager and Floor Team attempt to execute the floor maneuver within 3 minutes.

End of Game

1. Call time after 3 minutes or if the team successfully moves into "final" sequence.

2. Each Floor Team that successfully executes the floor move within the allowed time receives 25 points.

3. For multiple teams, the team that completes the floor maneuver in the shortest time wins.

● POST-GAME DEBRIEFING

Processing this exercise focuses on three separate, but related issues:

- *Planning.* Because those who do the planning are not those who must execute the plan, it's a safe bet that there will be issues that will be overlooked, ignored, or forgotten entirely. This being the case, groups can discuss the following:

  - What information do planners need in order to anticipate the needs of those who must implement?

  - How do planners and implementers need to interact in order to develop the most effective and realistic plans?

  - What aspects of implementation are planners most apt to overlook?

  - If planners could ask implementers three critical questions, what would they be?

  - What "lessons learned" do planners need to gather and share as implementation goes forward?

- *Floor Management.* Floor Managers and others who must translate plans into action are invariably left wondering, "What were they thinking?" "What did they assume?" and "Where do I need to stick to the plan and where do I have some wiggle room to improvise to fit reality?"

Engage Floor Managers in discussing:

- What was made clear in the plans and what remained a mystery?

- How did the Planners make your job easy and how did they make it more difficult?

- What do you wish the Planners had done to make the job of implementation easier?

- Where did the Planners seem to draw the boundaries between "their" job and "your" job? Was this a useful distinction or did it cause problems?

- *Floor Team.* Those who must implement the plans invariably face a reality different from that imagined by the Planners. Time, circumstance, change, new players—all these factors alter the task as imagined. This requires those who must implement not only to read and interpret instructions, but also to become active problem solvers in their own right. Engage the Floor Team in discussing:

  - What was the gap between the plan you were given and the constraints you actually had to contend with? What was the impact of this gap?

  - To what extent do you think it was clear what everyone was supposed to do (and why)? Where it was not clear what people were supposed to do, and what was the result?

  - As you were given implementation instructions, what do you wish you had known about the planning process, the people who did the planning, and the information they had available?

A wrap-up question for all participants is, "What did you learn about the planning process and how to improve it?"

● GENERAL COMMENTS

- This is an excellent way to introduce the elements of team planning and execution—through a simulation in which the roles of Planner, Floor Manager, and Floor Team implement the plan.

- Floor Managers may find it helpful to number the spaces on the floor grid with the nine blank index cards, as follows:

1	2	3
4	5	6
7	8	9

They can then direct their Floor Team to move to specific spaces "by the numbers."

● CUSTOMIZING FLOOR PLAN

Size of Group

- For groups of eight to fifteen, play as one team, assign additional players to the Planner and Floor Manager roles, as well as Observer and Recorder.

- For larger groups, assign two or more teams. Conduct the planning and meeting periods simultaneously. For the floor maneuvers, depending on the size of the room and time restrictions, consider one of the following:

  - Allow competing teams to observe each other. Discuss the value of "benchmarking" during the debriefing period.

  - Allow competing teams to observe each other, but require any observing team to complete its maneuver in less time than its predecessors (for example, say, "You must beat your predecessor by 20 seconds").

  - Require the non-playing Floor Teams and Floor Managers to leave the room while the other Floor Teams are completing their maneuvers.

  - Create multiple grids on the floor and then with the help of assistant monitors, equipped with a stopwatch (one for each grid), conduct the maneuvers simultaneously.

Time of Play

- Shorten or lengthen the time of play, depending on the skill level and size of your group. Because of the additional noise and confusion, larger groups usually require a planning round of 10 minutes.

Method of Play

- Repeat the exercise using more difficult designs after the group has successfully completed the first design. This allows the group to demonstrate the skills they learned in the first maneuver.

- For higher skilled groups:

  Obstructed Space. In the three-by-three configuration, assign one space as obstructed or off-limits—no player may stand in, move through, or end up in this space. This adaptation is especially effective if given as a last-minute ("special notice from the front office") type of instruction. For example, after the "X" and "O" Teams have conferred, but before they begin their floor moves, announce that one of the unused spaces (middle bottom or #8) has been designated "obstructed." Debrief in terms of rules that are put on teams and managers that limit or restrain their effectiveness. You may want to lengthen the planning round to 7 minutes. (See Solution: Obstructed Space.)

  Four-by-Four. Have four players from each team occupy the grid and move to an assigned final sequence. The use of only one free space requires additional planning and inter-team cooperation. Lengthen the planning round to 7 minutes. (See Solution: Ten Moves.)

  Lowest Bid. Have each team submit a "bid" on how much time it will take their Floor Team to complete the maneuver. The team with the "lowest" bid wins.

Scoring

- Award 25 points for any team that successfully completes the floor maneuver.

- Award 15 points for the team that successfully completes the floor maneuver in the shortest time.

Floor Plan

- Form teams of eight or more players.

- The team selects the subteams:

    The Planner creates the floor plan.

    The Floor Manager prepares the floor grid and coordinates/communicates all moves with the Floor Team.

    The Floor Team executes all moves on the floor grid.

- The Floor Team assembles on the floor grid.

- The Floor Manager and Floor Team have 3 minutes to complete the maneuver on the floor grid.

PLANNER INSTRUCTION SHEET FOR
Floor Plan

∙ ∙

You Will Receive These Supplies

1. Planner Instruction Sheet.

2. Starting/Ending Design Sheet.

3. Directions Sheet.

4. One set of planning markers—three red and three white.

You have 5 minutes to create a floor plan (strategy) to change your Floor Team—move-by-move—from "Starting Design" to "Ending Design" on the floor grid. By the end of the 5-minute planning period, you must develop a Directions Sheet for your Floor Manager.

Rules of the Move

1. Only one player may move at a time.

2. A player may not move outside the grid.

3. A player may move horizontally, vertically, or diagonally.

4. Two players may not occupy the same space.

5. A player may only move in two ways:

- Move into an adjoining open space OR

- Jump over a player of the opposite designator if there is an open space on the other side of the player.

Sample Jump Move

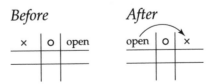

After 5 minutes you must deliver a copy of the Directions Sheet to your Floor Manager.

Good luck!

Games That Boost Performance. Copyright © 2005 by John Wiley & Sons, Inc. Reproduced by permission of Pfeiffer, an Imprint of Wiley. www.pfeiffer.com

FLOOR MANAGER INSTRUCTION SHEET FOR
Floor Plan

• •

You Will Receive These Supplies

1. Floor Manager Instruction Sheet.

2. Set of "X" and "O" cards.

3. Nine blank 5-inch x 8-inch index cards.

You have five minutes to prepare your floor grid and practice floor maneuvers with your Floor Team. By the end of the 5-minute planning period you must:

• Prepare a floor grid for the maneuver.

1	2	3
4	5	6
7	8	9

• Assign the "X" and "O" cards to your Floor Team.

• Practice floor maneuvers with your Floor Team.

During the Maneuver the Floor Manager

1. May talk to any player on the Floor Team, as required.

2. May NOT touch any member of the Floor Team.

3. May NOT enter the floor grid at any time.

Rules of the Floor Move

1. Only one player may move at a time.

2. A player may not move outside the grid.

3. A player may move horizontally, vertically, or diagonally.

4. Two players may not occupy the same space.

5. A player may only move in two ways:

- Move into an adjoining open space OR

- Jump over a player of the opposite designator if there is an open space on the other side of the player.

Sample Jump Move

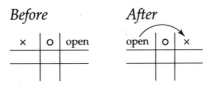

After receiving the Directions Sheet, you have 2 minutes to receive and then clarify any instructions with the Planner.

After the meeting with the Planner, you have 3 minutes to complete the maneuver.

Good luck!

FLOOR TEAM INSTRUCTION SHEET FOR
Floor Plan

•••

You Will Receive These Supplies

1. Floor Team Instruction Sheet.

2. Set of "X" and "O" cards (assigned by Floor Manager).

You are the operational team that will make your team's planning a success. Each of you will receive a designator card, marked with an "X" or an "O."

You will have 5 minutes to work with your Floor Manager on the following:

- Prepare the floor grid for the maneuver, as directed by the Floor Manager.

- Receive your assigned "X" and "O" cards.

- Practice floor maneuvers with your Floor Manager.

During the Maneuver Floor Team Members

1. May talk with other Floor Team members on the floor grid.

2. May NOT trade designator cards with any other player.

3. May NOT talk to the Floor Manager.

Rules of the Floor Move

1. Only one player may move at a time.

2. A player may not move outside the grid.

3. A player may move horizontally, vertically, or diagonally.

4. Two players may not occupy the same space.

5. A player may only move in two ways:

- Move into an adjoining open space OR

- Jump over a player of the opposite designator if there is an open space on the other side of the player.

Sample Jump Move

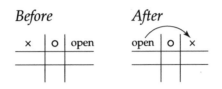

Once your Floor Manager completes his or her meeting with the Planner, you have 3 minutes to successfully complete the maneuver.

Good luck!

DIRECTIONS SHEET FOR
Floor Plan

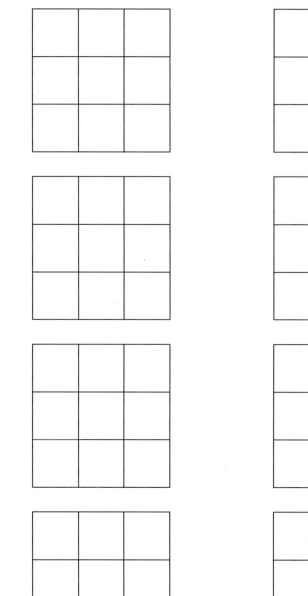

SOLUTION IN FIVE MOVES FOR
Floor Plan

Starting Design				Ending Design		
×	O	O		O	□	×
□	×	O	→	O	□	×
□	□	×		O	□	×

Move 1	×	O	O
	O	×	□
	□	□	×
Move 2	×	O	□
	O	×	□
	O	□	×
Move 3	□	O	×
	O	×	□
	O	□	×
Move 4	O	□	×
	O	×	□
	O	□	×
Move 5 (End Move)	O	□	×
	O	□	×
	O	□	×

SOLUTION IN TEN MOVES FOR
Floor Plan

· ·

Starting Design				**Ending Design**		
×	○	○		○	×	×
×	×	○	→	○	□	×
□	×	○		○	○	×

Move 1	× ○ □ × × ○ ○ × ○	Move 6	□ ○ × ○ × × ○ × ○
Move 2	× ○ × × □ ○ ○ × ○	Move 7	○ ○ × ○ × × ○ × □
Move 3	× ○ × □→× ○ ○ × ○	Move 8	○ ○ × ○ × × ○ □→×
Move 4	× ○ × ○ × □ ○ × ○	Move 9	○ □ × ○ × × ○ ○ ×
Move 5	× ○ × ○ □→× ○ × ○	Move 10	○ × × ○ □ × ○ ○ ×

SOLUTION IN SIX MOVES WITH OBSTRUCTED SPACE FOR
Floor Plan

	Starting Design			Ending Design	
✕	O	✕	O	□	✕
✕	O	□	O	□	✕
□	**	O	O	**	✕

Move 1	✕ O ✕ / ✕ □ □ / O ** O
Move 2	✕ O ✕ / ✕ O □ / O ** □
Move 3	□ O ✕ / ✕ O □ / O ** ✕
Move 4	□ O ✕ / □ O ✕ / O ** ✕
Move 5	□ O ✕ / O □ ✕ / O ** ✕
Move 6	O □ ✕ / O □ ✕ / O ** ✕

Floor Teams

● ●

● **PURPOSE**

- To demonstrate the importance of prior planning in effective problem solving.

- To demonstrate how assumptions affect our ability to communicate effectively.

- To demonstrate the dynamics of self-directed teams.

- To demonstrate the value of "thinking on your feet."

● **GAME OBJECTIVE**

The set of teams that completes the required floor maneuver in the shortest time wins.

● **PLAYERS**

Six or more.

● **TIME**

Thirty-five to fifty-five minutes.

● **SUPPLIES**

- One roll of masking tape.

- Overhead projector (if using transparencies) or a newsprint flip chart and felt-tipped markers.

- One set of six 5-inch × 8-inch index cards for each set of teams.

- Two sets of six markers—three red and three white—for each set of teams.

- One set of two Instruction Sheets for each set of teams.

- One set of two Planning Grids for each set of teams.

- Paper and pens/pencils for each team.

- Noisemaker (optional).

● PREPARATION

Create a floor grid (three-by-three Tic-Tac-Toe grid) as follows:

- Using masking tape, outline a six-foot square on the floor.

- Divide this square into two-foot sections, creating a three-by-three grid.

Using six of the 5-inch × 8-inch index cards, create a set of three "X" and three "O" cards for each set of teams by marking the letter "O" or "X" on both sides for easier identification.

Find "markers" for team planning. The markers can be red and white chips, brown and white chess pawns, felt-tipped marker tops, or even red and white dice. (*Note:* the two colors do not have to be the suggested red and white.)

● GAME PLAY

1. Divide the group into sets of two floor teams, three players to a team.

2. Have each team select a designator—the "X" floor team or "O" floor team.

3. Distribute one set of three "X" and three "O" cards to each team.

4. Have each team select an on-floor leader. The "X" and "O" on-floor leaders are responsible for directing their teams' on-floor maneuvers. They also meet with the other team leader, as necessary.

5. Distribute the Instruction Sheets and Planning Grids to each team.

6. Give the two leaders 5 minutes to meet with their teams and to review the Instruction Sheet.

7. After 5 minutes, have each team take its assigned grid spaces.

8. Inform each set of teams that they have 3 minutes to move to the "final" sequence.

9. Call time after 3 minutes or when the teams complete the floor maneuver.

10. Post the final sequence on the flip chart or overhead projector.

● POST-GAME DEBRIEFING

Floor Teams is an excellent way to demonstrate the real-time dynamics of self-directed teams. To introduce these dynamics you can ask:

- It's not enough for a team to plan its own moves; those moves need to be coordinated with other teams or other parts of the organization. What was easy or difficult in coordinating your movements with the other team?

- What tools or techniques did you use to create a common and shared vision of what needed to be done?

- Why is it hard to see the options available when you are right in the middle of the action?

- How long does a strategy last when people begin to get frustrated in trying to accomplish a task?

- What are the different ways that team members contribute to success?

- Why and when is it vital to include someone other than those immediately involved in developing a plan or strategy?

- How can capturing lessons learned help improve team performance?

- What happens when someone offers an idea or suggestion and it "plops" (no one responds or captures the idea or suggestion)?

Floor Teams is an excellent way to make the point that planning is a critical element of problem solving. Typically, most teams leap into problem solving long before they think about and come to agreement on:

- The roles that must be played within the team.

- How to select people for those roles.

- The assumptions that are being made about the task.

- How the team defines the problem.

- What needs to be communicated and with whom.

- How to stop and regroup if the team reaches an impasse.

As a result, teams can bury themselves so far down in the weeds that it is difficult for them to stop, reassess their situation, and then generate options for change. If participants become frustrated during the game (and they are very apt to do so if the team hasn't clearly agreed on its strategy in advance), the facilitator should step in and ask:

- What is happening right now?

- What is your strategy?

- What is getting in the way of pursuing that strategy?

- What assumptions are you making?

- If you were to question your assumptions, what new options might you consider?

● GENERAL COMMENTS

- If, as a facilitator, you see that teams are getting stuck in this situation, call a time out and inquire if either team has established a reference for the floor grid to help them with its maneuver. If neither team has created this reference, then introduce this simple grid pattern to help both teams plan and execute their floor moves:

1	2	3
4	5	6
7	8	9

● CUSTOMIZING FLOOR TEAMS

Size of Group

- For groups of ten or fewer, play as one team, assigning additional players to roles such as "observer" and "recorder."

- For larger groups:

  - Play separate rounds of one set of teams while other players observe. Each new round consists of a different starting and final assignments on the game grid. When teams observe others in play, they have a greater appreciation for communication procedures of preplanning.

  - Conduct simultaneous exercises on multiple game grids. Playing multiple grids may increase competition.

Time of Play

- Shorten or lengthen the time for a round of play, depending on the difficulty of the puzzle or the level of the audience.

Method of Play

- For easier play, simplify the requirements of the game by removing the "obstructed space." Easier play can be used for lesser skilled groups OR to practice floor maneuvers with your teams before you introduce the "obstructed space."

- For higher skilled groups, introduce the four-by-four maneuver (see Solution: Ten Moves.)

Scoring

- Award 25 points to each set of teams that make the correct moves within the prescribed time.

PLAYER INSTRUCTIONS FOR

Floor Teams

- Form two teams of three players—the "X" Team and the "O" Team.

- Each team selects a Team Leader.

- Each team receives a set of three "X" or three "O" cards.

- Each team receives Team Instructions, a Planning Grid, and a set of markers.

- Each team meets for 5 minutes to plan the floor maneuver.

- The players from each team assemble on the floor grid.

- Each set of teams has 3 minutes to reassemble in the final sequence.

FLOOR TEAM X INSTRUCTIONS FOR
Floor Team

. . . .

Supplies

- One Instruction Sheet.

- One Planning Grid.

- Six markers (three red, three white)

You have 5 minutes to meet and plan a simple floor maneuver that requires you to cooperate with your fellow "O" Team. Team "O" is known as cooperative and eager to work with other teams in the organization. During the maneuver:

- Players can only communicate with their own Team Leader.

- The "X" and "O" Team Leaders may communicate with each other as necessary.

Your first assignment is to learn the "rules of the move":

1. Only one player may move at a time.

2. A player may not move outside the grid.

3. A player may move horizontally, vertically, or diagonally.

4. Two players may not occupy the same space.

5. A player may only move in two ways:

- Move into an adjoining open space OR

- Jump over a player of the opposite designator if there is an open space on the other side of the player.

Sample Jump Move

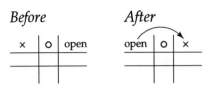

Your assignment is to complete the following maneuver. Note that the center space is obstructed, which means that no player from either team is allowed to enter or cross over this space.

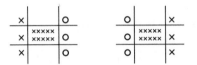

You may wish to use the markers and Planning Grid to plan your move.

Good luck!

FLOOR TEAM O INSTRUCTIONS FOR
Floor Team

· ·

Supplies

- One Instruction Sheet.

- One Planning Grid.

- Six markers (three red, three white).

You have 5 minutes to meet and plan a somewhat complicated floor maneuver that requires you to cooperate with your fellow "X" Team. Team "X" is known as a bit "reluctant" and unwilling to work with other teams in the organization. During the maneuver:

- Players can only communicate with their own Team Leader.

- The "X" and "O" Team Leaders may communicate with each other as necessary.

Your first assignment is to learn the "rules of the move."

1. Only one player may move at a time.

2. A player may not move outside the grid.

3. A player may move horizontally, vertically, or diagonally.

4. Two players may not occupy the same space.

5. A player may only move in two ways:

- Move into an adjoining open space OR

- Jump over a player of the opposite designator if there is an open space on the other side of the player.

Sample Jump Move

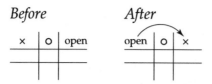

Before   *After*

Your assignment is to complete the following maneuver. Note that the center space is obstructed, which means that no player from either team is allowed to enter or cross over this space.

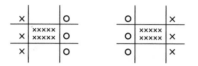

You may wish to use the markers and Planning Grid to plan your move.

Good luck!

PLANNING GRID FOR
Floor Teams

SOLUTION IN TEN MOVES WITH OBSTRUCTED SPACE FOR
Floor Teams

Start	X □ O		**Finish**	O □ X	
	X ** O - - - - ->			O ** X	
	X □ O			O □ X	

Move 1	X □ O	Move 6	O □- - ->X
	X ** O		X ** O
	X O<- -□		O □ X

Move 2	X □ O	Move 7	O X X
	X ** O		□ ** O
	□ O X - - - ->		O □ X

Move 3	X □ O	Move 8	O X X
	X ** O		□ ** □
	O<- -□ X		O O X

Move 4	□- - ->X O	Move 9	O □ X
	X ** O		□ ** X
	O □ X		O O X

Move 5	O<- -X- - -□	Move 10	O □ X
	X ** O		O ** X
	O □ X		O □ X

SOLUTION IN TEN MOVES FOR
Floor Teams

Start	×	○	○	**Finish**	○	×	×
	×	×	○ ⟶		○	□	×
	□	×	○		○	○	×

Move 1	×	○	□	Move 6	□	○	×
	×	×	○		○	×	×
	○	×	○		○	×	○

Move 2	×	○	×	Move 7	○	○	×
	×	□	○		○	×	×
	○	×	○		○	×	□

Move 3	×	○	×	Move 8	○	○	×
	□ ⟶ ×		○		○	×	×
	○	×	○		○	□ ⟶ ×	

Move 4	×	○	×	Move 9	○	□	×
	○	×	□		○	×	×
	○	×	○		○	○	×

Move 5	×	○	×	Move 10	○	×	×
	○	□ ⟶ ×			○	□	×
	○	×	○		○	○	×

Friendly Persuasion

· ·

● PURPOSE

- To explore common expectations as we interact with others.
- To demonstrate the value of personalization, friendliness, questioning, and persistence.
- To provoke a discussion of the cultural expectations within an organization and what constitutes "expected" behavior.

● GAME OBJECTIVE

To collect as many dots as you can on your "Player Card."

● PLAYERS

Eight or more.

● TIME

Twenty to fifty minutes.

● SUPPLIES

- One set of ten or more colored dots for each player (red, yellow, blue, or green).
- One 3-inch × 5-inch index card for each player.

- An overhead projector (if using transparencies) or a newsprint flip chart and felt-tipped markers.

- An "Award Criteria" card for each player.

- Pens to personalize each player's dots.

- Felt-tipped markers to personalize each player's "Player Card."

● PREPARATION

Prior to the game, create as many "Award Criteria" cards as you will have participants. For each participant, copy one of the criteria from the Award Criteria Sheet onto a 3-inch × 5-inch index card. You can also create your own criteria.

● GAME PLAY

1. Hand out one index card, an Award Criteria card, and a pen or pencil to each player. Place felt-tipped markers in an accessible place.

2. Have players write "Player Card" on the top side of the index card and then their names underneath the title.

3. Tell players that they are free to decorate or personalize their cards with the felt-tipped markers and pens.

4. Distribute a set of colored dots to each player.

5. Have each player mark or initial his or her colored dots.

6. Explain that players have 10 minutes to collect dots from other players and that the player with the most dots when time is called wins.

7. Explain the following rules:

    - Every player must show his or her "Player Card."

    - A player may only collect one dot from any other player.

    - Players only receive dots if they comply with the "Award Criteria."

    - Players may not share the contents of their "Award Criteria" with other players.

    - Players who receive dots are NOT obligated to award one in return.

8. Start game play.

---

9. Call time after 10 minutes.

10. The player with the most dots wins.

● POST-GAME DEBRIEFING

Friendly Persuasion helps participants articulate their assumptions about the "right way" to do things, as well as the "wrong way" to get things done.

In any organization, there is some version of the question, "What does it take to get a dot around here?" To provoke that debate, you might ask:

- What is the equivalent of a "dot" in your organization?

- How does this organization or team distribute "dots"?

- What are the rewards for doing what is expected?

- How does this organization punish or exclude those who do not accrue the normal dots?

- What ARE the expectations around here for someone who "knows how to behave"?

- What are the cues that you have failed to understand or meet expectations?

- What alternatives do you have for uncovering and understanding unwritten expectations?

- What's the RIGHT way to ask for what you need around here?

- What's the WRONG way to ask for what you need? What are the consequences of asking the WRONG way?

Often we make sense of what we experience by talking it over with others. Swapping lessons learned is one means by which we learn faster and more effectively. To process these lessons, you might ask:

- Did you take the opportunity to talk over your experiences with someone else?

- Did you ask questions of the other players?

- What led you to ask questions or decide not to ask questions?

- How might you ask questions in the workplace to more quickly figure out what is going on and what rules apply?

● GENERAL COMMENTS

- Friendly Persuasion is an excellent way to demonstrate the many "agendas" that prevail in the work environment. This game can be used to remind players that certain traits, such as friendliness (offering a handshake or saying, "Hello"), personal touches (decorating your own player card), and persistence (receiving a dot ONLY after being refused) pay off in small, and sometimes large, ways.

- In any culture (whether it begins with a family, a club, a church, a gang, or an organization) expectations evolve about the "right" way to greet others, show interest, present oneself, and ask for what one wants or needs. Because the majority of these rules or expectations are unwritten, we often don't become aware of them until we omit one, violate one, or ignore the cues that we need to behave differently.

● SAMPLE PLAY

1. Sixteen players receive their Instruction Sheets, Award Criteria cards, Player Card, pens, and ten colored dots.

2. Each player prepares the "Player Card" and initials his or her colored dots.

3. The players are given 10 minutes to collect their dots.

4. Player One approaches Player Two.

   - Player One presents his Player Card and says, "How are you?"

   - Player Two's instructions are to award a dot to any player who initiates contact and offers a greeting.

   - Player Two awards a dot to Player One.

   - Player Two then asks Player One for a dot.

   - Player One's instructions are to award a dot to any requesting player.

   - Player One awards a dot to Player Two.

5. Player Three approaches Player Four.

   - Player Three presents her card, smiles, and offers a handshake to Player Four.

- Player Four's instructions are to award a dot only to players who have decorated their Player Cards. Player Three's card is not decorated.

- Player Four does NOT award a dot to Player Three.

- Player Four then offers his card to Player Three.

- Player Three's instructions are to award a dot to players who have been refused once.

- Player Three does NOT award a dot to Player Four.

- Player Four asks again.

- Player Three awards a dot to Player Four.

● CUSTOMIZING FRIENDLY PERSUASION

Size of Group

- For larger groups of twenty-five to fifty, play as described, but allow more time for the size of the group.

Time of Play

- Shorten or lengthen the time allowed for presentations and votes, depending on the size of the group.

Method of Play

- Have players form small groups and then, as a group, approach other players to request dots on each group member's individual Player Card. Discuss how group collecting differs from individual collecting.

- Have players form teams and develop a team Player Card. Discuss how a team's Player Card differs from an individual's card.

Scoring

- Have players award an extra dot to other players who seem to make an exceptional request. Discuss the concept of "primacy," the ability to make excellent first impressions.

PLAYER INSTRUCTIONS FOR
Friendly Persuasion

∙∙

- **Receive a blank index card, an Award Criteria card, a pen, and a sheet of colored dots.**

- **Write "Player Card" and your name on the index card.**

- **Initial your colored dots.**

- **Approach other players, seeking one of their dots for your "Player Card."**

- **You may only collect one dot from any one player.**

- **The player with the most dots wins.**

AWARD CRITERIA FOR
Friendly Persuasion

. . . .

Award Your Dot Only If the Applicant . . .

- Says a greeting such as "Hello!" or "How are you?"
- Makes eye contact and smiles.
- Asks again, after being refused the first time.
- Comments on something that you are wearing.
- Shows respect by bowing or nodding his or her head.
- Extends his or her hand as if to shake your hand.
- Is NOT wearing anything that is red in color.
- Is female.
- Is male.
- Wears eyeglasses.
- Is wearing something brown.
- Does not make you feel "rushed."
- Wears a necklace, neck chain, or bracelet.
- Has decorated his or her Player Card.
- Offers to trade you a dot for a dot.
- Allows you to ask for a dot before he or she asks for a dot.
- Is someone you don't know.
- Is someone you know.
- Asks about your card and the lessons you have learned in collecting dots with this group.
- Offers to assist you in gathering dots from others.
- Warns you to keep away from those who refuse to give dots.
- Asks if you would be interested in jointly collecting dots (that is, asking someone, "Could you please spare a dot for my friend here?).

Ghostwriter

· ·

● PURPOSE

- To expand a group's technical, functional, or organizational vocabulary.

- To reinforce key concepts or principles.

● GAME OBJECTIVE

To score the most team points.

● PLAYERS

Nine or more.

● TIME

Thirty to sixty minutes.

● SUPPLIES

- One sheet of flip chart paper, masking tape, and felt-tipped markers.

- Ten or more sets of nomenclature cards containing a key item or term.

- An overhead projector (if using transparencies) or a newsprint flip chart and felt-tipped markers.

- One set of Ballot Sheets for each team.

- Index cards and pencils.

- References and manuals (to verify concepts and terminology).

● PREPARATION

Develop sets of three nomenclature cards—3-inch × 5-inch index cards or half sheets of paper—one card stating the term and definition and the other two cards stating the term and the statement: "You have 2 minutes to create a definition for the term . . ."

Create at least one set of cards for each team for each round of play. If you have three teams and plan to conduct three rounds of play, you would require nine sets of nomenclature cards.

To create the Ballot Sheets, photocopy the ballots found at the end of this game. Using the above example—three teams for three rounds—you would need two sheets per presentation (presenting team does not require a ballot) for a total of nine presentations × two sheets (to the voting teams), totaling eighteen Ballot Sheets. Note that the Ballot Sheet is formatted two to a page; thus nine photocopies cut in half equals the eighteen sheets needed for the game.

● GAME PLAY

1. Divide group into two or more teams of three or more members per team.

2. Seat each team at its own conference table.

3. Have each team select a team name.

4. Distribute index cards, Ballot Sheets, and pencils to each team.

5. Have each team write its team name on its Ballot Sheets.

6. Have each team select three players to serve as "ghostwriters," whose job is to write definitions for the nomenclature cards.

Round 1

1. Select the first team to present.

2. Distribute a set of three nomenclature cards to the presenting team.

One card contains the item and the correct definition.

The other two cards contain the item and state: "You have 2 minutes to create your own definition."

3. Tell the presenting team members they have 2 minutes to write their definitions.

4. Call time at the end of 2 minutes.

5. Ask the first team to present the three definitions to the other teams.

6. Each observing team(s) meets for 2 minutes and then selects one of the three definitions.

7. The observing teams submit their selection on a Ballot Sheet to the facilitator.

8. If the observing team selects . . .

The *correct* definition, the observing team receives 5 points.

An *incorrect* definition, the presenting team receives 3 points.

9. The facilitator records the scores on the flip chart or overhead.

10. Select the next team to present.

Play is the same for all presentations and all rounds.

11. Declare the team with the most points the winner.

● POST-GAME DEBRIEFING

Ghostwriter is a novel way to not only reinforce existing vocabulary, terms, or concepts, but to engage participants' imagination and sense of humor as well. By challenging teams to not only come up with the correct definition, but also to make up plausible alternatives, they discuss the context we use to make sense of and apply both terms and concepts.

After you announce the correct answer and award points, ask teams:

- Why is this term important?

- How does it relate to your job?

- To what extent is this term or concept "loaded" in the sense that it carries political or cultural overtones? How does that affect how it is used in your organization?

- For whom else in the organization is this term important? Why is it important to him or her?

- What about this term or concept can be confusing?

- How is it that you knew the meaning of this term or concept?

- What strategy did you follow in generating your alternate definitions? What did you consider to make your definition seem plausible?

- In your organization, what do people do to make sure that everyone is "on the same page" in their understanding of terms and concepts?

- Would you say that most people in your organization speak a mutually understandable language or do different teams and groups use terminology that is a mystery to everyone else? What is the cost when we don't really understand each other?

● GENERAL COMMENTS

- To develop your own set of key terms or concepts, begin with "need to know" information typically included in new hire orientations and new product demonstrations. You can also use Ghostwriter to familiarize staff with a new customer account, stakeholder issues, or key operating principles. It is an ideal game to orient employees to commonly used acronyms, trade-specific nomenclature, or mechanical parts or subsystems of equipment.

- To engage groups immediately, start with terms that you can safely assume most of the group will know or guess. After that, progress to less-well-known terms, but make sure that you don't turn this into a game of Trivial Pursuit.®

- Use terms or principles that have day-to-day value or impact on the ability to perform effectively as a member of this organization or team. Suggested items for the nomenclature cards:

  - Use lesser-known trade acronyms and abbreviations.

  - Introduce the organization's new products.

  - Introduce product lines of competing organizations.

  - Use organizational abbreviations used by personnel, production, operations, etc., to ensure they are known and understood.

- Introduce computer acronyms.

- Play lively and energetic music while the ghostwriters are "composing." This covers the sound of discussion as writers come up with their alternative definitions and can also be used as a time marker (select music in 2-minute segments).

● SAMPLE PLAY

Preliminaries

1. Divide the group into two teams—Team A and Team B.

2. Each team selects three ghostwriters.

3. Team A receives a set of nomenclature cards.

3. Team B signs its name on its Ballot Sheet.

Round 1

1. Team A's ghostwriters receive a set of three cards with "ISBN" written on it.

   - One ghostwriter receives the card with the definition: "The definition of ISBN is: International Standard Book Number."

   - The other two ghostwriters receive cards stating: You have 2 minutes to create a definition for the acronym ISBN."

2. Team A's ghostwriters prepare two alternate definitions.

3. After 2 minutes the ghostwriters of Team A present three definitions:

   - *Choice 1:* Independent Strategic Business Networks

   - *Choice 2:* International Standard Book Number

   - *Choice 3:* Improved Scientific Behavioral Norms

4. After some discussion, Team B selects Choice 1.

5. Team B's selection was incorrect—the correct response was Choice 2, so the presenting team, Team A, receives 3 points.

6. Play alternates.

● CUSTOMIZING GHOSTWRITER

Size of Group

- For groups of six to ten, play as two teams.

- For larger groups of twenty-five to fifty, form no more than five teams. Make sure each team gives as many of its members a chance to be a "ghostwriter" as possible.

Time of Play

- Shorten or lengthen the time allowed for presentations and votes, depending on the size of the group.

- Allow more time, such as 5 minutes, for the creation of definitions.

Method of Play

- After the third round, cut the time allowed for "ghostwriting" by 30 seconds until the teams are down to 30 seconds to develop alternate definitions.

- Allow ghostwriters to access books or manuals to help them create the definitions.

- Give the ghostwriters the definitions and let them create the name of the item. This might be especially helpful for new product launches.

Scoring

- Award bonus points if a team can provide additional information beyond the definition.

- Award bonus points for the most creative, humorous, unique, or provocative definitions or presentations.

PLAYER INSTRUCTIONS FOR
Ghostwriter

· ·

- **Divide into two or more teams.**

- **Each team selects three ghostwriters.**

- **Each ghostwriter receives a nomenclature card—one card has a definition, the other two cards are blank.**

- **The two ghostwriters with blank cards have 2 minutes to create definitions.**

- **The first team presents its three definitions.**

- **If the observing team selects . . .**

    The *correct* definition, it receives 5 points.

    An *incorrect* definition, the presenting team receives 3 points.

- **The team with the most points wins.**

BALLOT SHEET FOR
Ghostwriter

Our Team Name _____   Item _____

☐ Definition #1

☐ Definition #2

☐ Definition #3

BALLOT SHEET FOR
Ghostwriter

Our Team Name _____   Item _____

☐ Definition #1

☐ Definition #2

☐ Definition #3

Hard Case

· ·

● PURPOSE

- To create dialog about topics where there is no one, easy answer.

- To challenge players to put principles into practice.

- To develop players' skills in surfacing and identifying their assumptions.

● GAME OBJECTIVE

To be the first team to reach "finish."

● PLAYERS

Eight to thirty players.

● TIME

Thirty-five to sixty minutes.

● SUPPLIES

- Set of five or more case studies about the topic, developed by the facilitator. (See Hard Case Sample Case Study for an example.)

- One Game Chart drawn on the flip chart or presented on an overhead transparency.

- One set of icons for tracking each team's progress on the Game Chart.

- A set of Answer Sheets for each team.

● PREPARATION

Case Studies

For each case study develop three different "levels" of correct responses: "most appropriate," "second most appropriate," and "least appropriate." One variation in scoring is to use four alternatives. This variation requires you to double up or assign two of the responses as equal value—such as two choices ranked "second most appropriate" OR two choices ranked "least appropriate."

As you develop each case, make a note of what you consider to be the important reasons why one response is "more" or "less" correct than other responses. These reasons might include existing legislation, rules, procedures, or practices; cultural values; ethical considerations; mechanical implications (if you do . . . , it is apt to have what sort of impact on . . .); or relationship "ripples." To the extent possible, rank these considerations in your own mind so that you will be prepared to discuss these points as team members raise them.

Game Chart

Newsprint. Draw the Game Chart on a sheet of flip chart paper. Advances up the Game Chart can be indicated by movable icons made of paper, index cards, or small Post-it® Notes OR by filling in a track's spaces with felt-tipped markers.

Overhead transparency. Reproduce the Game Chart on an overhead transparency. Use markers, such as coins or paper clips, to indicate advances up the chart.

Answer Sheets

Prepare a set of Answer Sheets, one for each team. For each set, there should be as many sheets as there are cases to be presented. To save paper and time there are two Answer Sheets placed on each page. Simply photocopy and cut.

● GAME PLAY

1. Divide the group into two or three teams.

2. Have each team select a number track (1, 2, or 3) on the Game Chart.

3. Place each team's icon on the Game Chart.

4. Distribute one Answer Sheet to each team.

Round 1

1. Present the first case study.

2. Give each team 5 minutes to record its response on the Answer Sheet.

3. After 5 minutes, have each team presents its response to the rest of the group.

4. Present the correct responses—the "most appropriate," then the "second most appropriate," and then the "least appropriate," with elaboration, as needed.

5. Scoring: If the team's response is . . .

   The *most appropriate,* advance the team's icon three spaces on the Game Chart.

   The *second most appropriate,* advance the team's icon one space on the Game Chart.

   The *least appropriate,* do not move the team's icon.

6. Repeat the same procedure for all rounds.

7. The first team to cross into the "finish" area wins. (If no team has crossed into the "finish" when the allotted time expires, the team closest to "finish" is declared the winner.)

● POST-GAME DEBRIEFING

In processing Hard Case some portion of your audience will expect a clear right and wrong answer for every question. There will also be some relativistic thinkers who can see both sides to every question and answer. In processing any case, you may want to ask:

- What is the most important consideration in this situation?

- What were the pros and cons you identified in arriving at your chosen answer?

- What was it about this particular case that was difficult or problematic?

- What argument or logic persuaded your group to go with the answer you chose?

- To what extent are most questions on the job a matter of judgment rather than a clear black or white, right or wrong answer?

- How do people apply judgment on the job to arrive at their answers?

- What are the factors that typically cause us to accept one answer and reject all others?

- Which is more prized on your team, the ability to see all sides of a question or the ability to arrive at a clear, definitive answer?

- What did you learn about your own decision-making process by playing this game?

- When you were challenged on your answer, how did you explain your rationale?

- By what process did your group finally agree on your answers?

    Did you vote?

    Let the loudest voice win?

    Build a consensus?

    Or use some other means to agree?

● GENERAL COMMENTS

- This is an excellent "visual" way to review the topic with the entire group. The Game Chart creates a "race" game environment. By introducing more challenging question formats, such as a mini-case study with three or four responses, you can acquaint participants with the group-problem-solving process, give them immediate feedback on their decision in a "game show" environment, and help them gain an understanding of the decision-making process and critical thinking.

- Most important issues are rarely black and white. Making a judgment call about Hard Case is a matter of distinguishing among varying shades of gray and weighing the pros and cons of any one of a number of different actions and decisions. Hard Case promotes that ability to look at all the different aspects of a problem and perspectives of those involved in order to arrive at a "better" decision—even if a "perfect" decision is not clear.

- Hard Case encourages teams to seek input from everyone in the group. This can be reinforced during closure when you ask each team how it came up with its ideas. Inevitably, the team or teams with the most progress up the track will reveal that they asked everyone for input. The game demonstrates that players can provide input in differing ways. The more extroverted players may initially take charge but turn to shyer members for contributions as the game evolves.

● SAMPLE PLAY

1. The group is divided into three teams.

2. The facilitator has each team select a track on the Game Chart:

   - Team A selects Track 1.

   - Team B selects Track 2.

   - Team C selects Track 3.

3. The facilitator has prepared five scenarios; therefore, she hands out one set of five Answer Sheets to each team.

Round 1

1. The facilitator presents the *first* case study: Email Privacy:

   "One of your employees reports that the computer in the work area next to her is receiving offensive material, including pornographic pictures, and wants you to monitor the offending employee's messages.

   "Which of the following is the most correct?

   "*Choice A.* You may always read your employees' messages because the company provides the computers to the employees.

   "*Choice B.* You may read any messages only if the company provides for the email system.

   "*Choice C.* You may never read an employee's email."

2. Each team records its response on an Answer Sheet.

3. The facilitator collects one Answer Sheet from each team.

4. The facilitator presents the correct response.

- Team A selected "b," the most appropriate response, and advances three spaces.

- Team C selected "a," the second most appropriate response, and advances one space.

- Team B selected "c," the least appropriate response, and stays put.

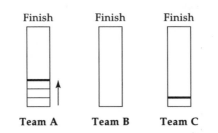

5. The facilitator discusses the reasons for the ranking of the choices.

6. This ends play for Round 1.

Round 2

1. The facilitator presents the second case study.

2. Each team records its response on the Answer Sheet.

3. The facilitator collects one Answer Sheet from each team.

4. The facilitator presents the correct response.

- Teams B and C had the most appropriate response.

- Team A had the least appropriate response.

5. The facilitator advances the icons for Teams B and C three spaces and leaves Team A's icon on the third space.

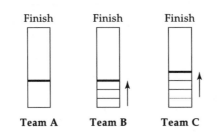

6. This ends play for Round 2.

Rounds 3 to 5

1. Play continues in this fashion until the facilitator has presented five scenarios.

2. The first team to cross into "finish" wins.

3. If time runs out, the team that has advanced the farthest on the Game Chart is declared the winner.

● CUSTOMIZING HARD CASE

Size of Group

- Divide smaller groups into two or three teams.

- Divide larger groups into five teams. You will need to add two tracks to the Game Chart. Be sure to allow for more time to discuss and evaluate the listed items and be sure to review the results of the game with the entire group.

Time of Play

- Shorten or lengthen the time for a round of play depending on the difficulty of the question material or the understanding level of the group.

- Expand or contract the number of rounds of play.

- Conduct as a "whole course" game by continuing play in the succeeding modules.

Method of Play

- Create several sets of questions in different topics. Allow the teams to select the next topic.

- Assign one or more case studies as a take-home exercise and then, in the next session, conduct the game using several of the case studies assigned.

Scoring

- At present, the Game Chart has twelve steps for advancing the icon. You can shorten or lengthen the amount of game play by simply shortening or lengthening the Game Chart.

- Create a multiple-choice question format and award three spaces for the most correct, one space for the second most correct, and no spaces for the least correct.

- Create a case study offering four choices, making sure that at least two choices receive the same number of spaces—choice 1: advance three spaces, choice 2 and choice 3: advance one space, and choice 4: stay put.

- Create a set of "RISK" questions where the icon moves UP a specified number of spaces for a correct response and DOWN for an incorrect response.

Hard Case

....

- **Form two or three teams.**

- **Each team selects a track on the Game Chart.**

- **The facilitator presents a case study.**

- **Record your response on the Answer Sheet.**

- **Scoring: If your response is . . .**

    Most Appropriate, **your icon is advanced three spaces.**

    Second Most Appropriate, **your icon is advanced one space.**

    Least Appropriate, **your icon stays put.**

- **The first team to reach finish wins.**

GAME CHART FOR
Hard Case

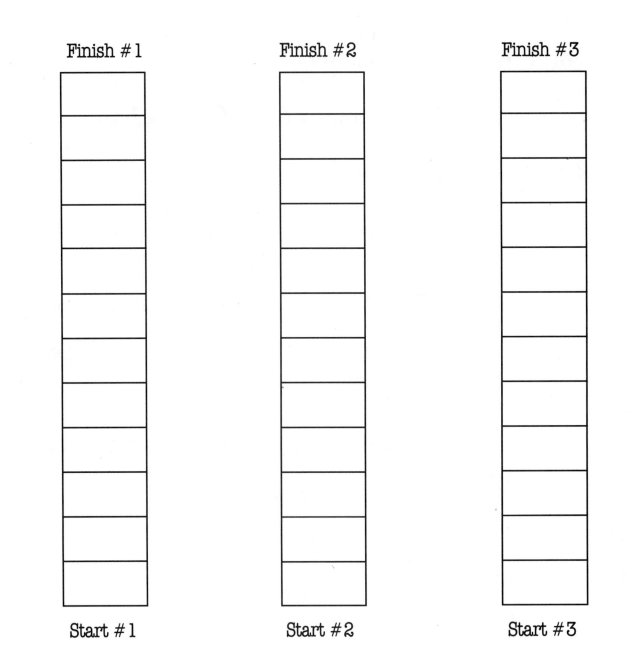

Finish #1   Finish #2   Finish #3

Start #1   Start #2   Start #3

ANSWER SHEET FOR
Hard Case

. . . .

Team Name _____

Case Study # _____

☐ Choice #1

☐ Choice #3

☐ Choice #2

☐ Choice #4

ANSWER SHEET FOR
Hard Case

. . . .

Team Name _____

Case Study # _____

☐ Choice #1

☐ Choice #3

☐ Choice #2

☐ Choice #4

Hard Case

. . . .

Email Privacy

One of your employees reports that the computer in the work area next to her is receiving offensive material, including pornographic pictures, and wants you to monitor the offending employee's messages.

Which of the following is the most correct?

a. You may always read your employees' messages because the company provides the computers to the employees.

b. You may read any messages only if the company provides the email system.

c. You may never read an employee's email.

Choice b = Most Appropriate, advance three spaces.
(If messages are maintained on a system provided by the employer.)*

Choice a = Second Most Appropriate, advance one space.
(If employee has a separate email, the rights of the employer are more limited.)*

Choice c = Least Appropriate, stay put.
(This approach could create a liability for the company. Company may want to advise employees that it maintains the right to monitor the system, which should discourage misuse.)*

*Federal Employee Communications Privacy Act.

Having a Bad Hair Day

● PURPOSE

- To surface common annoyances in a team setting and negotiate protocols to avoid these annoyances.

- To identify aspects of organizational culture that commonly get in the way of optimum team performance.

- To creatively discuss how to diffuse stress in the workplace.

● GAME OBJECTIVE

To collect the most team points.

● PLAYERS

Nine or more.

● TIME

Fifteen to thirty minutes.

● SUPPLIES

- One sheet of flip chart paper and felt-tipped markers for each team.

- Newsprint flip chart and felt-tipped markers to track the voting.

- An overhead projector (if using transparencies).

- One index card per player.

- Paper and pencils.

- Masking tape.

- Timer (optional).

- Noisemaker (optional).

● GAME PLAY

1. Divide participants into three or more teams of three to seven players per team.

2. Distribute paper and pencils to each player.

3. Have each player record one or two annoying events he or she experienced in the past week. (Remind players not to identify specific people.) Provide some examples from the List of Annoying Events if you choose.

4. Call time after 1 minute.

5. Distribute one sheet of flip chart paper and felt-tipped markers to each team.

6. Have players join their teams and share their annoying events.

7. Have each team . . .

   (a) Select its most common or top-ranking annoyance and

   (b) Produce a list of creative responses to avoid, eliminate, or mitigate this annoyance.

8. Call time after 7 minutes.

   Then give each team another 3 minutes select the five most creative ways of dealing with the annoying event.

Team Presentations

1. Have each team present its event and the five most creative ways for dealing with it and then post its chart paper on the wall.

2. Distribute one index card to each player.

3. Have each player select his or her favorite creative response from any OTHER team's list.

Scoring

1. After 3 minutes, call time and collect the ballots.

2. Award 1 point for each selected response.

3. The team's response that receives the most votes wins.

● POST-GAME DEBRIEFING

Having a Bad Hair Day is also an opportunity to introduce the "Question Behind the Question"—that is, when we ask "who, "when, or "why" questions, what we are really asking is permission to play the victim. When we ask "Who is responsible?" we are getting into the blame game rather than focusing on "What can we do about this situation to fix it?" When we ask, "When is this going to be resolved?" we are avoiding the question, "How can I act to do something about it right now?" When we ask "Why me? Why us? Why is this horrible thing happening?" what we are really asking is "How long shall we continue to wallow in glorious self-pity?" There are really only two responsible questions:

- "What can I do to help?"

- "How can I make a difference right now?"

For Facilitators with Advanced Group Skills. Have groups develop responses to one or more annoying experiences that are specific to this group. Use the discussion to "clear the air" of some underlying issues or logistical problems facing the group.

Having a Bad Hair Day is one way to shine a light on the choices we make about assuming personal responsibility and accountability for doing what needs to be done and our thinking process about how to make a difference in a particular situation. Here are some questions to stir up that conversation:

- When you encounter an annoyance, how many of you typically decide to

  Ignore it?

  Call the problem to someone else's attention?

  Write a complaint?

  Call to complain?

Deal directly with the person causing the annoyance?

What are the pros and cons of each of these choices?

- When you are annoyed at someone else, are you more likely to

Blame it on him or her?

Blame it on the system?

Wonder whether it is just a matter of miscommunication?

Blame it on yourself?

Take it on yourself to straighten this person out?

What are the pros and cons of each of these choices?

- Annoyances are, for the most part, a function of not getting what we expected to get. To what extent do you find that your colleagues:

Have a good grasp of each other's responsibilities?

Understand what gets in the way of satisfying others?

Take time to negotiate expectations?

Capture (in writing) what each person is supposed to do?

- As you compared your reactions with those of others on your team, would you say that you typically:

Underreact to the situation?

Overreact to the situation?

Act appropriately, given the provocation?

- What we choose to do in any given situation is a function of what we see as being within our control, within our influence, or outside our control or influence.

What situations did you see as being within your control?

What situations did you see as being within your sphere or influence?

What situations did you see as being outside your control or influence?

What are your strategies for dealing with situations you neither control nor influence?

● GENERAL COMMENTS

- Having a Bad Hair Day is an excellent way for intact work teams to uncover petty annoyances and to deal with them in an open and humorous way. As you debrief the game, you can focus the group on identifying practical solutions to these petty annoyances. By generating a basic list of annoyances— "pet peeves" if you will—groups can create protocols to avoid annoying each other unnecessarily as they go about their tasks.

- Having a Bad Hair Day can be used to explore the "hidden elephant" aspects of organizational culture that annoy many people, but which they feel powerless to change. A hidden elephant is a problem that is apparent to everyone, but which everyone is reluctant to discuss. For example, an organization that considers itself "prudent" may, in fact, be pathologically averse to risk in any form whatsoever. An organization that prides itself on being "flexible" may, in fact, be incapable of following through on any given plan and strongly resist sustained commitment in any form.

- Introduce some perspective on the relative importance of some annoyances by building on humorous and creative responses to underscore that perhaps, just perhaps, we may overact to petty annoyances. For example, one participant responded to "being cut off in traffic" by "calling in an air strike." The group savored this moment and then concluded that traffic headaches, while annoying, were petty compared to other real-world problems.

● CUSTOMIZING HAVING A BAD HAIR DAY

Size of Group

- For groups of six to ten, divide into two teams. Have players vote for any favored response from either team. Facilitator may serve as tiebreaker, as required.

- For larger groups of twenty-five or more, play as prescribed, but allow additional time for the presentations and voting periods.

Time of Play

- Shorten or lengthen the time for a round of play depending on the size of the audience.

- Shorten the top number of creative responses to three.

- Lengthen the top number of creative responses to seven.

Method of Play

- Create an ongoing list of annoying events. Write each event on a card, place the cards in a container, and have each team select one of the "bad hair cards" to build its responses around.

- Select one common annoying event, either from past group input or from your own personal list. Have teams create lists of creative responses to the event.

- Create a wall chart of annoying events. Allow players to record an ongoing list of their creative reactions and other remarks during breaks.

- Have all the teams select one common event. Have each team present its list of responses and then have the players select the most humorous, creative, or appropriate response.

- Have groups move to another team's posted responses and develop additional responses to the list.

- Use this exercise as a fun way to get into more serious problems of work site and plant safety, personal and team conflict, computer security, and so on.

- Post a list of "favorite annoying events" and encourage participants to add their own favorites. From the final list select two or three favorites and produce a list of creative responses. (See List of Annoying Events.)

Scoring

- Award bonus points for the presenter who most convincingly presents his or her team's list of responses.

- Change the scoring system.

  - *Dots.* Issue one red dot and one blue dot to each player. Have players use these dots to award "first choice" (red) and "second choice" (blue). Tally the points by multiplying all first choices by 5 points and all second choices by 3 points. The team with the most total points wins.

  - *Chips.* Issue one red and one white chip to each player. Have players deposit their chips into a paper cup or container underneath each specific response. Tally the points the same as above.

Having a Bad Hair Day

- **Divide into three or more teams.**

- **Players record one or more annoying events.**

- **Teams select one event and produce five creative responses.**

- **Teams present the event and list of responses to the entire group.**

- **Players vote for their favorite response.**

- **The team with the response that receives the most votes wins.**

LIST OF ANNOYING EVENTS FOR
Having a Bad Hair Day

Here are sample events you can reference or use to give your players a jumping off point:

- Getting Cut Off in Traffic
- Gridlock
- Out of Coffee
- Someone Parking in Your Parking Space
- Locking Keys in Your Car
- Wrong Telephone Number at Midnight
- SPAM
- Bad Email Protocol
- Inconsiderate Neighbors (Noisy)
- Litterbugs
- Unruly Children in Public Places
- Dogs Off the Leash
- Facial Jewelry
- Tattoos
- Men in Baggy, Baggy Pants
- Slow Restaurant Service
- Cell Phones While Driving
- Cell Phones in Public Places
- Boom Boxes in Public
- Loud Car Stereos
- Unattended Barking Dogs
- Cursing in Public
- Spitting in Public
- People with Attitudes
- Whining Children
- Misbehaving Children in Public Places
- Cars with Muffler Problems
- Elvis-Itis
- People with No Life

The Hello Effect

••

● PURPOSE

- To demonstrate that it's not just what you say, but how you say it that counts.

- To promote dialog about the effect of managerial behavior on a workplace environment.

● GAME OBJECTIVE

To score the most team points.

● PLAYERS

Nine or more.

● TIME

Twenty to forty-five minutes.

● SUPPLIES

- One sheet of flip chart paper, masking tape, and felt-tipped markers.

- A newsprint flip chart and felt-tipped markers.

- One set of three Mood Cards for each team, prepared in advance by the facilitator.

- Six Response Sheets for each team (assuming three rounds and three teams; if more of either, then more Response Sheets will be needed).

- An overhead projector (if using transparencies).

- One Score Sheet, shown on flipchart or overhead.

● GAME PLAY

1. Divide into three teams of three or more players each.

2. Distribute three Mood cards to the first team.

3. Distribute a Response Sheet to each of the other two teams.

4. Teams select one card and a presenter.

5. The presenting player must say:

   "Hello, how are you doing today?" in the mood presented on the card.

Team One

1. The Team One representative player presents a greeting.

2. The other two (observing) teams have 1 minute to guess the mood. They may ask the presenter to repeat the greeting.

3. Both observing teams write down the mood and three characteristics portrayed during the greeting onto the Response Sheet.

4. Collect the Response Sheets.

Scoring

1. For each observing team that identifies the correct mood the . . .

   Observing team receives 15 points.

   Presenting team receives 25 points.

2. For each characteristic matched by the two observing teams, both observing teams receive 5 points.

3. Facilitator records the scores on the flip chart.

4. This completes play for Round One.

Teams Two and Three

1. Play is the same for each presentation.

2. Play continues in this fashion until teams have presented all of their Mood Cards or facilitator calls time.

3. The team with the most points is declared the winner.

● POST-GAME DEBRIEFING

The Hello Effect is an excellent way to demonstrate that "It's not WHAT you say but HOW you say it." Some participants may not be aware of the effect normal day-to-day conversations have on recipients. As the game proceeds, players may discover a distinct disconnect between what was "meant" and what was "heard." This game offers players an interesting way to discover differing perspectives between what was said and what was meant. The following questions help spur the discussion:

- As you think back on how the presenter said, "Hello," what did you weigh most heavily?

  Inflection?

  Expression?

  Body posture?

- When there is a "disconnect" between what someone says and their tone, posture, or expression, which do you tend to believe?

- How do you determine the difference between someone who "wants to be your friend" and someone who "wants a favor from you"?

- Does your boss routinely say "Hello" first thing in the morning?

- How important is it to you that the boss greet you in the morning?

- What do you listen for if he or she does say "Hello"?

- What, if any, effect does how the boss says "Hello" have on the office?

- How do you judge the boss's mood?

● GENERAL COMMENTS

- Whether we intend it or not, what we think about others invariably leaks out, not only by what we say, but by how we say it. The purpose of this exercise is to sensitize people to the impact they have and the environment they create, even through such innocuous interactions as saying hello.

- In trying to guess the mood of the person in each exchange, participants are simply doing what we all do every day—use all available clues to help us understand what is going on around us and what we need to do to get along.

● CUSTOMIZING THE HELLO EFFECT

Size of Group

- For groups of six to ten, divide into two teams.

- For moderate groups of fifteen to thirty, play as described.

- For larger groups over thirty-five, play separate rounds of one set of teams while other players observe.

Time of Play

- Shorten or lengthen the time for a round of play depending on audience size and skill level.

Method of Play

- *Short Straw.* Have teams select their presenter in a random draw. (*Note:* If presenter is extremely reluctant, have group select another presenter.)

- Allow the observing teams to ask up to three questions of the presenting team—questions that can only be responded to by "yes" or "no."

- Have presenter introduce him- or herself to at least one member of each team.

Scoring

- Award bonus points for any presenter who convincingly or uniquely demonstrates the mood.

The Hello Effect

- **Divide into three teams.**

- **First team receives Mood Cards.**

- **Team selects one card and its presenter.**

- **Presenter says, "Hello," etc., in the mood shown on the card.**

- **The observing teams guess the mood and write down three characteristics of the greeting.**

- **Scores are awarded to both presenting team and observing teams for correct guesses.**

MOOD CARDS FOR
The Hello Effect

....

Each Mood Card should follow the template shown below.

Replace the "mood statement" with one of the items from the list below or from a description of your own choosing.

> Try to convey this mood to the other person as you say: "Hello, how are you doing today?"
>
> (Mood statement)

Mood Statements

- You are very late for a meeting and don't have time to chat.
- You are in a really foul mood.
- You do not want to talk to this person.
- You are really glad to see this person.
- You need to soften this person up before giving him or her bad news.
- You need to prepare this person prior to giving a criticism or correction.
- You are just being polite—going through the motions.
- You are trying to create an upbeat, positive tone to the day.
- You really admire this person.
- You are worried that this person is on edge or about to "blow up."
- You find this person amusing.
- You find this person annoying.
- You aren't sure whether this person is a friend or a foe.
- You want this person to like you.
- You want this person to fear you.
- You want to convey sympathy and emotional support.

RESPONSE SHEET FOR
The Hello Effect

• •

Our Team # _____   Presenting Team # _____

Mood demonstrated: _____

Three characteristics demonstrated:

      1. _____

      2. _____

      3. _____

RESPONSE SHEET FOR
The Hello Effect

• •

Our Team # _____   Presenting Team # _____

Mood demonstrated: _____

Three characteristics demonstrated:

      1. _____

      2. _____

      3. _____

Improbable Headlines

● ●

● **PURPOSE**

- To demonstrate the tendency to "fill in the blanks" when we are presented with incomplete corporate communications.

- To surface assumptions we make about organizational culture—the "story behind the story."

● **GAME OBJECTIVES**

- To create the most creative headline.

- To create the most ambitious headline.

● **PLAYERS**

Nine or more.

● **TIME**

Twenty to thirty-five minutes.

● **SUPPLIES**

- Set of Improbable Headlines, each on its own index card, enough for each team to receive five headlines. (See Sample Improbable Headlines sheet for some ideas.)

- An overhead projector (if using transparencies) or a newsprint flip chart and felt-tipped markers.

- Two index cards for each participant.

- Pens or pencils and paper for each participant.

- Masking tape.

● GAME PLAY

1. Divide the group into three teams of three to five players per team.

2. Seat each group at its own conference table.

3. Distribute five headlines to each team.

4. Distribute two index cards and pens or pencils and paper to each participant.

5. Each team has 10 minutes to select one headline and generate "the real story" behind its headline.

6. Call time after 10 minutes and have each team present its story to the rest of the group.

7. Have each player select the team's story that is the most creative and the one that is the most ambitious and write their choices on the index cards, one choice per card.

8. Tally the cards to determine which story received the most votes.

9. Announce the team that tallied the most in each category.

● POST-GAME DEBRIEFING

Once the scores are in and the winning stories have been announced, focus the group on what they have learned from this exercise. Ask:

- Back in the actual workplace, what do you wonder about when you read an official announcement or communication?

- Do you find yourself trying to read between the lines?

- What is your story about how things really work around here?

- What is the organization's track record in maintaining open communications with employees?

- When you aren't sure what's going on, to whom do you normally go for information or clarification? (*Note:* This is often NOT the boss—which should be an eye-opener for managers in the group.)

- What gives credibility to a story in your organization?

- If the upper echelons of management wanted people to put more faith in the information they put out, what should they do differently?

- Which has more credibility in your organization, information that is passed officially or that which comes down through the grapevine?

● GENERAL COMMENTS

- In any organization there is the openly published version of an event and then there is the "story behind the story" that explains what really (or probably) happened. The purpose of this exercise is to engage participants in a better understanding of their own organizational culture. Through debriefing, participants can discuss how they think it works and explore the commonly held myths about leadership, relationships, and policy. It is a wonderful way to point out to new leaders, supervisors, or managers the extent to which people will automatically fill in the details and make up an explanation when none is provided or when the story that is given out fails to conform with people's experience. This game has ample potential for humor and the only caution is that the "story" that people create to explain these headlines cannot openly defame any individual.

- Lead the applause after each presentation. Ask each team to rate the story that was just presented. They can give it 1 to 10 points for Creativity, and 1 to 10 points for Ambitiousness in capturing some aspect of generally recognized culture. Give teams 2 minutes to agree on their scoring. Ask each team to hold up their scorecard (sheet of paper), just as a judge might do at the Olympics, for each of the two areas rated. Keep track of these scores on a composite flip chart.

- The terms "creativity" and "ambitiousness" can be subject to interpretation. Develop ranking criteria for these terms or use this opportunity to have the group develop their own criteria.

● SAMPLE PLAY

Preliminaries

1. Divide group into three teams—Team A, Team B, and Team C.

2. Have each team select one headline from the five cards they receive.

3. Have each team create the "story behind the headline."

Team A: "Harvard Selects Company for Intern Program"

- Team member presents story of how a research paper created by one of their personnel staff was cited by the *Harvard Business Review* (HBR) for its insight and vision. HBR then sent out an interview team to discuss the paper with personnel. Based on their findings, the Harvard Business School selected the company for a one-year research study on how small business outperforms big business in personnel service to its employees.

Team B: "Accounting Quartet Appears on Star Search TV Program"

- Team member presents story of how a home video of the "Bottom Lines," the whimsical barber shop quartet from Internal Accounting, lead to an audition and subsequent appearance on the national TV program, "Star Search." Since the appearance, the quartet has had to go on extensive leave to accommodate requests, including an opening act for Cher in Las Vegas.

Team C: "Research & Development Invents Ultimate Firewall"

- Team member presents story of how the Information Systems Lab, teaming with R&D, created a hacker-proof firewall. After extensive testing, the company is considering offers from Dell, Microsoft, Macintosh, and Cisco in the private sector, plus contracts with GAO, Department of Defense, and Department of the Treasury.

Scoring

- The players mark their choices of "Most Creative" and "Most Ambitious" on their two index cards and submit the cards to the facilitator.

- Team B (Barber Shop Quartet) wins the "Most Creative."

- Team C (Firewall) wins the "Most Ambitious."

● CUSTOMIZING IMPROBABLE HEADLINES

Size of Group

- For groups of six to ten, play as two teams.

- For larger groups of twenty-five to fifty, form teams of five players each.

- Have teams select from two headlines.

- Have each team present the "story."

- Have players select first, second, and third favorites in each category.

- Collect and tabulate votes.

Time of Play

- Shorten or lengthen the time allowed for presentations and votes, depending on the size of the group.

- Allow more time for the story creation as required.

Method of Play

- Two-day workshop. Give headlines to teams at the end of the day and allow the teams to work on the stories overnight.

Scoring

- Ask players to pick first AND second favorites in each category—award 5 points for each first choice and 3 points for each second choice.

- Introduce other award categories, such as "most humorous," "most profound," "most shocking," and "most unique."

Improbable Headlines

- **Form three teams.**

- **Select one Improbable Headline and then generate the "real story" behind the headline.**

- **Present the headline and story to the group.**

- **Vote on the most creative and the most ambitious stories.**

SAMPLES FOR
Improbable Headlines

Here are sample headlines you can reference or use to give your players a jumping off point—just change the "company" to your corporate name and make other adjustments as necessary:

- Company Purchases Microsoft
- Robin Williams MCs Annual Awards Dinner
- Cafeteria Receives Julia Child Award
- Company Drinking Water Prolongs Life Expectancy
- Employee of the Month Wins Hawaii Vacation
- Suggestion Program Saves $100 Million
- Federal Reserve Lauds Economic Staff
- Bill Gates to Speak at Annual Picnic
- Retirement Program Is Model for Industry
- Wal-Mart Seeks Loan
- Company Buys General Electric
- Computer Analyst Solves Worldwide Virus
- R&D Team Wins Nobel Prize
- Congress Hails Company's War Effort
- R&D Discovers Fat Free, No Cholesterol Chocolate
- Coffee Service Receives the Starbucks Award
- Company to Host 2008 Olympics
- Company to Host 2008 Presidential Debates
- VP Marketing Leaves to Head Universal Studios
- Next Company Picnic: Disneyland
- Company Jingle Captures Grammy
- *Gentleman's Quarterly* to Do Feature on Company Dress Code
- Company Sponsored Halloween Costumes Featured on "Sixty Minutes"
- Cafeteria Pound Cake Wins Pillsbury Bake-Off
- Company Doubles Market Share

Initial Assumptions

- -

● **PURPOSE**

- To serve as a creativity warm-up prior to a brainstorming or problem-solving session.

● **GAME OBJECTIVE**

To score the most team points.

● **PLAYERS**

Eight or more.

● **TIME**

Twenty-five to sixty minutes.

● **SUPPLIES**

- Five Puzzle Sheets for each team for each round.

- An overhead projector (if using transparencies) or a newsprint flip chart and felt-tipped markers.

- Paper and pencils.

● PREPARATION

Using the blank Puzzle Sheet templates, create five puzzles for each round, using the samples provided or developing your own. Copy the Puzzle Sheet sets so that you have enough for each team.

● GAME PLAY

1. Divide the group into two or more teams of four to five players.

2. Have each team meet at a separate table.

3. Distribute the first set of five Puzzle Sheets.

4. Demonstrate one or more puzzles:

   - 16 O in a P—measurement (16 ounces in a pound).

   - 6 F in a L—measurement (6 fathoms in a league).

5. Instruct each team they have 3 minutes to solve all five puzzles.

6. After 3 minutes collect each team's Puzzle Sheet.

   - If all five responses are correct, the team receives 15 points.

   - If one or more response is incorrect, the team receives 2 points for each correct response.

Subsequent Rounds

1. Play for three to six rounds.

2. The play is the same for all rounds.

3. The team with the most points is declared the winner.

● POST-GAME DEBRIEFING

Discussion questions might include:

- What was the hardest part of getting started?

- Who was tempted to solve it by themselves rather than work collaboratively? What impact did this have on the team?

- Who had the first breakthrough? How easy or difficult did the person find it to get the team's attention?

- What process did your team use to figure out the meaning of the puzzle? What sorts of things did you discuss?

- Did you find it useful to write down possibilities, or did you simply rely on your collective memory?

- Who in your group was most useful in this exercise? What characteristic or talent made them most useful?

- Would that same talent be as useful in solving workplace puzzles? In what way?

- What did you have to know about a subject in order to make a reasonable guess at the meaning of the puzzle?

- What are ways in your organization that you could more effectively clue people in so that they could understand sometimes-puzzling behavior or events?

● GENERAL COMMENTS

- This is a good "limbering up" exercise prior to a focused problem-solving session because Initial Assumptions encourages participants to think laterally in order to decipher the clues provided. It also reinforces the role that pattern recognition plays in helping us make sense of what we see, hear, and experience.

- This exercise can be used to stimulate discussion of the many ways in which team members contribute to problem solving. Some of us have a propensity for remembering statistical trivia (such as the number of fathoms in a league) or an ability to extrapolate a pattern (30 days hath September, April, June, and November) or an ability to compose fragments into a whole (such as reconstituting vanity license plates into the phrase or idea they express—RBRDUQ is rubber duck). After one or two rounds, teams will identify which of their members are most resourceful, most imaginative, know the most facts, or are most willing to guess. A useful processing point is to ask, "How did you identify the talent inherent in your team and what did you do to tap that talent?"

- Post one or two puzzles on the wall following a break. Players often return early to see what new puzzles are offered.

- *Learning Point:* It's not always obvious what we are looking at or supposed to see unless we have some context for making sense of it. In properly orienting new people to an organization, it's just as important to provide them with a context for understanding what they see as it is to provide facts about the organization. Context provides a framework that enables us to interpret what we see and experience in ways that build our knowledge and understanding.

● SAMPLE PLAY

1. Divide the group into three teams.

2. Distribute the first set of Puzzle Sheets.

   > 10 = A in the B of R (government)
   > 26 = L in the A (language)
   > 12 = S of the Z (science)
   > 2,000 = P in a T (measurement)
   > 30 = D hath S, A, J, and N (miscellaneous)

3. After 3 minutes collect the completed Puzzle Sheet from each team.

4. Team A has three correct responses:

   - 26 letters in the alphabet.

   - 2,000 pounds in a ton.

   - 30 days hath September, April, June, and November.

5. Team A receives 2 points for each correct response.

   Team A receives 2 points × 3 for a total of 6 points.

6. Team B has four correct responses:

   - 10 amendments in the Bill of Rights.

   - 26 letters in the alphabet.

   - 12 signs of the zodiac.

   - 2,000 pounds in a ton.

7. Team B receives 2 points for each correct response.

   Team B receives 2 points × 4 = 8 points.

8. Team C has all 5 correct responses:

- 10 amendments in the Bill of Rights.

- 26 letters in the alphabet.

- 12 signs of the zodiac.

- 2,000 pounds in a ton.

- 30 days hath September, April, June, and November.

9. Team C receives 15 points.

10. Scoring for Round 1:   Team A = 6 points;

Team B = 8 points;

Team C = 15 points.

Subsequent Rounds

1. All rounds are played in a similar fashion.

2. The team with the most points wins.

● CUSTOMIZING INITIAL ASSUMPTIONS

Size of Group

- Divide smaller groups into two teams.

- Divide larger groups into teams of five. Alternate Puzzle Sheets as a way to discourage players from eavesdropping on other teams' problem solving. Allow for more time to discuss and evaluate the listed items and be sure to review the results of the game with the entire group.

Time of Play

- Shorten or lengthen the rounds of play—shorten to 2 minutes, lengthen to 4 minutes—depending on the difficulty of the clues or level of the audience.

- Play additional rounds to ensure coverage of team play and communication issues.

- Allow additional time for larger groups to deal with general issues of game play.

Method of Play

- Create puzzles that cover organizational topics and acronyms.

- Have players create puzzles for future rounds of play. This gives you a perspective of what they see in a puzzle as well as helping you fill your "puzzle bank."

- Add an "outsourcing model" to the game play by allowing any team to "sell" a clue—anything that helps but does not solve the puzzle—to any other team for 1 point for each clue. The receiving team MUST pay 1 point, whether or not the clue helps them solve that specific puzzle.

- Suggested questions for "outsourcing" post game debriefing . . .

  - What led to your decision to buy or not to buy clues?

  - If your team decided to buy a clue what did you hope you would receive?

  - How did the clues you purchased help you think about possible answers?

Scoring

- Award 3 points for each solution and a bonus of 10 points for solving all of the puzzles.

- Award an all-or-nothing score of 15 points for the solution of all puzzles, but 0 points for four or fewer solutions. Discuss how this all-or-nothing approach reflects the real world.

- Impose a penalty of minus 10 points for any team not solving all of the puzzles. Discuss how this penalty approach reflects the real world.

Initial Assumptions

- **Form two or more teams.**

- **You have 3 minutes to solve a set of five puzzles.**

Scoring:

- **If all puzzle solutions are correct, you receive 15 points.**

- **If one or more puzzle solutions are incorrect, you receive 2 points for each correct solution.**

SAMPLE PUZZLE SHEET FOR
Initial Assumptions

Team Name _____   **Round** _____

10 = A in the B of R (government)   _____

26 = L in the A (language)   _____

12 = S of the Z (science)   _____

2,000 = P in a T (measurement)   _____

30 = D hath S, A, J, and N (miscellaneous)   _____

Here are sample puzzles you can use in your game play or to help you create your own.

Puzzles	**Solutions**
8 P in a G (measurement)	8 pints in a gallon
46 P of the U.S. (history)	46 presidents of the U.S.
50 S in the U.S. (geography)	50 states in the U.S.
3 G in a H T (sports)	3 goals in a hat trick
52 W in a Y (measurement)	52 weeks in a year
12 M in a Y (measurement)	12 months in a year
7 G W of the W (history)	7 great wonders of the world
1,000 G in a K (measurement)	1,000 grams in a kilogram
12 I in a F (measurement)	12 inches in a foot
3 F in a Y (measurement)	3 feet in a yard
20 Y in a S (measurement)	20 years in a score
42 G in an oil B (measurement)	42 gallons in an oil barrel
9 J in the S C (government)	9 justices in the Supreme Court
3 P C—R, B, and Y (miscellaneous)	3 primary colors—red, blue, and yellow
5 P on a B T (sports)	5 players on a basketball team
4 + 20 BB B in a P (nursery rhyme)	4 and 20 black birds baked in a pie
3 B M, S H T R (nursery rhyme)	3 Blind Mice, See How They Run
100 U for a DC (book title)	*100 Uses for a Dead Cat*
GL and the 3B (fairy tale)	*Goldilocks and the Three Bears*
15 M on a D M chest (literature)	*15 Men on a Dead Man's Chest* – yo ho ho . . .
J and the B S (fairy tale)	*Jack and the Bean Stalk*
27 A in the C of the U.S. (government)	27 amendments in the Constitution of the U.S.

PUZZLE SHEET FOR
Initial Assumptions

• •

Team Name _____

Round _____

(Puzzle)

(Solution)

_____

_____

_____

_____

_____

PUZZLE SHEET FOR
Initial Assumptions

• •

Team Name _____

Round _____

(Puzzle)

(Solution)

_____

_____

_____

_____

_____

Listen Up

● ●

● **PURPOSE**

- To demonstrate the focus and energy required in active listening.

- To create a dialog about what constitutes good listening.

● **GAME OBJECTIVE**

To score the most points.

● **PLAYERS**

Eight or more.

● **TIME**

Fifteen to twenty-five minutes.

● **SUPPLIES**

- One Team Worksheet for each team.

- One or more sets of tasks and solutions, prepared in advance for verbal presentation (see Samples I and II).

- An overhead projector (if using transparencies).

- One flip chart or chalkboard for scoring or feedback.

- Stopwatch and noisemaker (optional) to be used to call time.

● GAME PLAY

1. Divide group into teams of two players each.

2. Distribute one Team Worksheet to each team.

3. Inform players that you will be orally delivering directions to tasks that require their undivided attention.

4. Say that each task—mathematical or logical—requires a written response.

   Players are NOT allowed to take any notes or make any computations.

5. When instructed, players are to write their responses on the worksheet.

6. Team members may SILENTLY confer before writing the response.

7. Inform the players that you will be presenting ten tasks.

8. Ask each team to estimate how many tasks it will correctly answer.

   Post the estimates on the flip chart or overhead transparency.

9. Present each task, allowing 15 seconds for team responses.

10. Go over the correct responses.

    Award 1 point for each correct response.

11. Have each team tally its score. The team whose score matches or exceeds the original estimate wins.

● POST-GAME DEBRIEFING

Ask teams to identify and discuss the strategies they used to help them "listen up." You may wish to ask:

- On what basis did you make your estimate of your listening skills?

- Whose actual score came close to your estimated score?

- Whose actual score was off from your estimated score?

- How often do you need to hear information repeated before it sinks in? (*Note:* Most of us need at least two or three repetitions, whether this is internal or external repetition.)

- What tricks or techniques do you rely on to help yourself remember what you have heard?

- How something is said often affects our ability to listen well. How would you have preferred to hear the information provided?

- How do you help yourself eliminate distractions when it is important that you listen well?

The following teaching point can be made after the game is debriefed:

- How often have you been introduced to someone only to draw a complete blank when you want to call him or her by name 30 seconds later? All of us fall prey to distracted listening at one time or the other. This exercise is an excellent way to promote understanding of what focused listening actually involves. At a minimum, focused listening involves one or more of the following strategies:

  - Engaging one or more sense systems in listening—looking at the speaker, making notes, counting on your fingers, and other methods.

  - Repetition and reinforcement (repeating silently in your head what you just heard or "playing it back" aloud).

  - Association (mentally linking what you have just heard with some clue or content that will help trigger your memory of what was said).

  - Visualization (creating a mental image of what has been said or described, for example, visualizing a string of numbers, creating a mental map of directions, attaching a name to a face with an imaginary nametag).

● GENERAL COMMENTS

- Most of us think of ourselves as excellent listeners. In point of fact, what most of us hear is strongly influenced by what we are expecting to hear, what we want to hear, how much of our attention is focused on the speaker, questions we are waiting to ask, and our internal thoughts about the information being presented. Often the way information is presented impedes our ability to listen well. Some of us prefer an overview first and then details, and others prefer to hear the details first and then the summary last.

- Because of these tendencies, this game includes an "estimate" of skill. For people to really focus on their listening abilities, it is important that they estimate their score and then receive immediate feedback on their actual performance. As in life, it is sometimes really instructive to get the test before you receive the lesson. Failure to do as well as you think you will do is a powerful attention grabber. Player feedback indicates that many "listeners" were amazed at how ineffective their listening style was.

- To summarize, the steps of active listening include focus, asking questions, and resisting distractions.

CUSTOMIZING LISTEN UP

Size of Group

- For groups of four to six, play as two or three teams.

- For larger groups of twenty-five to fifty:

  - Take additional time, as required, to post examples of pre-game estimates and post-game scores.

  - If you have to split the group into two rounds of play, then assign the teams sitting out the round to observe one of the playing teams, then reverse the roles on the second round. Debrief what behaviors the observing teams noted during the rounds of play.

Time of Play

- Shorten or lengthen the time allowed for presentation of the tasks, depending on the difficulty of the computation.

- Present five computations to shorten the game play.

Method of Play

- Prepare a set of ten mini directions or oral instructions of fewer than thirty-five words on almost anything, such as:

  - Geographic directions (take the first left, then go one mile . . .).

  - Medical procedures (to provide a tourniquet, first . . .).

- Computer instructions (to log into the M27 program, first . . .).

- Technical descriptions (the 47B modular board requires . . .).

- Recipes (fold one egg into a standing mixture of . . .).

- Corporate data (HQ in Toledo, with twenty-seven divisions in seven countries).

- Safety regulations (no open containers of F7 cleaners are allowed in . . .).

- Read the first description and then immediately ask the listener a specific question (How far did you travel after taking the first left? [1 mile]).

Then read the second description, followed by the question, and so forth.

- The dynamics of "listen only, no notes" requires absolute attention to the topic in the form of a game.

- Prepare two worksheets and answers to ensure that you have two rounds of play for larger groups. Also, some past groups have asked to play a second round for practice and for the fun of it.

Scoring

- Perfect Score Bonus:

  Perfect Score = 3 bonus points

  One Incorrect Response = 1 bonus point

- To simplify scoring, eliminate the estimate and announce that the team with the highest score (number of solved puzzles) wins.

PLAYER INSTRUCTIONS FOR
LISTEN UP

- Divide into teams of two.

- Each team estimates how many items it will solve.

- Each team listens to each item and then writes down its response.

- Each team tallies its correct responses.

- The team whose score matches or exceeds the original estimate wins.

SAMPLE I FOR
Listen Up

• •

1. Start with 8; double it; add 5; divide by 3; your answer is _____. (7)

2. Start with 11; subtract 5; add 4; add 6; divide by 4; your answer is _____. (4)

3. Start with 13; add 10; add 2; divide by 5; multiply by 6; add 3; divide by 3; your answer is _____. (11)

4. From a number that is 4 larger than 11, add 6; divide by 3; subtract 2; your answer is _____. (5)

5. From a number that is 2 smaller than 10, add 6; add 4; multiply by 2; divide by 3; divide by 4; your answer is _____. (3)

6. Add 6 to 11; subtract 8; add 9; subtract 13; double it; your answer is _____. (10)

7. Add 7 to 5; add 6; add 7; add 5; add 6; divide by 4; your answer is _____. (9)

8. Subtract 7 from 11; add 5; multiply by 5; subtract 15; subtract 10; add 1; your answer is _____. (21)

9. From a number that is 6 larger than 7; add 2; add 3; divide by 6; multiply by 4; add 3; your answer is _____. (15)

10. Take the square root of 16; add 9; add 11; divide by 4; add 3; divide by 3; your answer is _____. (3)

Listen Up

. . . .

1. Start with 7; double it; add 4; divide by 3; your answer is _____. (6)

2. Start with 9; subtract 4; add 5; add 5; divide by 3; your answer is _____. (5)

3. Start with 15; add 9; add 2; divide by 2; multiply by 3; add 3; divide by 3; your answer is _____. (14)

4. From a number that is 4 larger than 12, add 5; divide by 3; subtract 4; your answer is _____. (3)

5. From a number that is 2 smaller than 10, add 7; add 6; multiply by 2; divide by 3; divide by 2; your answer is _____. (7)

6. Add 6 to 11; subtract 9; add 8; subtract 13; double it; your answer is _____. (6)

7. Add 7 to 5; add 4; add 3; add 2; add 1; divide by 2; your answer is _____. (11)

8. Subtract 7 from 11; add 1; multiply by 5; subtract 5; subtract 5; add 1; your answer is _____. (16)

9. From a number that is 6 larger than 7; add 5; add 2; divide by 4; multiply by 3; add 3; your answer is _____. (18)

10. Take the square root of 25; add 6; add 1; divide by 2; add 6; divide by 3; your answer is _____. (4)

TEAM WORKSHEET FOR
Listen Up

• •

Estimated Correct Responses _____

Correct Responses _____

1. _____

2. _____

3. _____

4. _____

5. _____

6. _____

7. _____

8. _____

9. _____

10. _____

Newscast

● **PURPOSE**

- To practice the skills of summarizing and capturing the essence of a story.

- To discuss what we see as important or trivial.

- To create a better understanding of key concepts involved in a given topic or situation.

● **GAME OBJECTIVE**

To score the most points.

● **PLAYERS**

Nine or more.

● **TIME**

Fifteen to sixty minutes.

● **SUPPLIES**

- One case study for each team per round (see Sample Case for example).

- One Guidelines Sheet for each player (presenting teams and target audience).

- One Team Presentation Ballot for the target audience and for the facilitator for each presentation.

- Reference material, such as a dictionary or technical journals, as needed.

● GAME PLAY

1. Select three players to be the "target audience." It is the job of the target audience to evaluate each presentation, in accordance with the Guidelines.

2. Divide the group into two or more teams.

3. Distribute the same case study or "breaking story" to each team.

4. Distribute a Guidelines Sheet to each participant.

5. Distribute one ballot to the Target Audience for each presentation.

6. Inform teams that they have 10 minutes to create a 60-second newscast on the forthcoming case study. Presenters can use only simple visuals or props.

7. During the 10-minute preparation period, the target audience should be discussing the criteria they will use to evaluate each presentation. They can use the criteria on the ballot or add their own items. Instruct the target audience that they need to agree on three criteria that will apply to all presentations. The target audience judges will award each presentation between 1 and 10 points for each criterion. The maximum any team can earn is 30 points.

8. After 10 minutes, call time.

9. Have each team select its newscaster.

10. Send the newscasters who are not presenting from the room during other teams' newscasts.

11. Have each team present its 60-second newscast.

12. After each presentation, give the target audience 2 minutes to make notes on the presentation.

13. After all presentations have been made, have the target audience meet and score each presentation on the criteria they have identified. Scores should be based on a 1- to 10-point scale for each criterion.

14. Complete your own form using the same criteria.

15. Combine the scores from the Target Audience and Facilitator Ballots and then tally the score received by each team.

16. The team with the highest score wins.

● POST-GAME DEBRIEFING

On one level, Newscast is about presentation skills, but it is also an opportunity to explore our own critical-thinking skills and the criteria we use to distinguish the "important stuff" from the "okay to ignore stuff." The following questions help guide that discussion:

- What was the hardest part of preparing your presentation?

- In our day-to-day work we don't get scoring feedback from our audiences. How is it we know when we succeed or fail to get our message across?

- As you read the case study, what criteria did you use to distinguish the important from the less important information?

- Did you attempt to anticipate the interests and concerns of your target audience? If so, how did you do that?

- When you are listening to an announcement in the workplace, what are you most interested in?

- As your team prepared its presentation, how did you choose what to include or leave out?

- Target Audience:

  - How did you select the criteria you decided to apply?

  - Did you weight the criteria at all?

  - Was one criterion more important than the others? If so, why?

- What did you learn from this game about the challenge of communication?

● GENERAL COMMENTS

- This is an excellent way to interactively introduce or reinforce any concept that can be written into a one-page study. Newscast can be used to support a wide range of communication topics and to provide practice in presentation skills. It also helps reinforce which aspects of your case students think are most important. Everyone must have said, at one time or another, that he or she could have done a better job on a news story. This brings real-time experience and pressure into background reading and case study material.

- Allow each team to select its newscaster. If you have more than one case study, insist that each team provide another newscaster for each case.

- Provide the target audience with guidelines to review during the preparation part of the game. A useful guideline might list the demographics of the target audience—age, number of members of the household, median income, gender, and so forth.

- Adding your score with the target audience's score takes some of the peer pressure off of them while adding expert validity to the score.

● CUSTOMIZING NEWSCAST

Size of Group

- For groups three to six, play as one team, with you serving as the target audience. (Although the students lose some of the "game atmosphere," the game still involves the students in the critical skills of assessing and presenting information.)

- For groups of seven to twelve, play as two teams with the two or three players serving as the target audience.

- For larger groups, distribute two sets of cases and play in two rounds—one group observing while the other group presents. By doubling the case studies you can cover more material.

Time of Play

- Shorten or lengthen the time for a round of play depending on the difficulty of the topic, length of the case study, or the level of the audience.

Method of Play

- Give each newscaster a "spin" or direction in which you want the audience swayed. Ask the target audience if they were persuaded by this story position.

- Use a 1-minute timer or large clock to create additional pressure on getting the story across before time expires.

- Add "glitz" with a news desk, extra lights, video cameras, and production staff, including a point-and-shoot director.

Scoring

- Award 5 bonus points if any newscast was able to persuade or sway the target audience.

Newscast

....

- **Facilitator selects a three-player "target audience."**

- **Divide into two or more teams.**

- **Each team receives a story.**

- **Teams prepare a 60-second group presentation on the story.**

- **The target audience and facilitator score each presentation.**

- **The team with the highest score wins.**

GUIDELINES FOR
Newscast

. . . .

1. Analyze the story

General Purpose

☐ Inform _____

☐ Persuade _____

☐ Entertain _____

Specific Purpose

☐ What do I want my audience to know? _____

☐ What do I want my audience to do? _____

☐ What do I want my audience to feel? _____

Audience Analysis

☐ Knowledge or experience with the topic _____

☐ Audience expectation or needs _____

☐ Attitude and concerns about the topic _____

2. Develop Content

Select Main Point

☐ "Must" know information—concepts, skills, or behaviors the audience must know, perform, or believe

☐ Main points—ideas that will guide the audience to understand or believe your point of view

Organize Main Point

☐ Purpose: I want my audience to know _____

☐ State main point or position _____

☐ Support main point or position _____

3. Conclusion

☐ Summarize main point or position _____

☐ Create sense of commitment or motivation (optional)

PRESENTATION BALLOT FOR
Newscast

• •

Team/Presenter's Name ————————————

Presentation Topic ————————————

Instructions: Prior to the presentations, check off the three criteria selected. After each presentation, write your score from 10 (high) to 1 (low) on the rule preceding the selected criteria.

———— ☐ Organization

———— ☐ Understandable Language

———— ☐ Audience Involvement

———— ☐ Informative

———— ☐ Motivating or Persuading

———— ☐ Entertaining

———— ☐ Other: ————————————————

———— ☐ Other: ————————————————

———— ☐ Other: ————————————————

———— ☐ Notes: ————————————————

Newscast

● ●

When Is a Scarf Not a Scarf?

Paris. July 4th. When Amelie Matahout earned her teaching certificate four years ago to teach the highly regulated French elementary school curriculum for science, she seemed to epitomize the classic immigrant success story. Born and schooled in Casablanca, Morocco, Ms. Matahout emigrated to Paris as a college student, graduating from L'Universite de Paris with honors in biology and chemistry. She married a French engineer, became a French citizen, and, at age 24, earned the credentials to teach anywhere in the French national system.

By the fall of 2001, she had built a reputation as a gifted, highly dedicated teacher with both the staff of her school and the parents of her students. In the wake of September 11th, Ms. Matahout made what became a significant decision. She began wearing a headscarf. School officials from the 15th Arondissement promptly suspended Ms. Matahout, maintaining that the headscarf could have a negative religious influence on the schoolchildren in her classroom. Their ultimatum was lose the scarf or lose your job.

Ms. Matahout sued and, in the two years since her case was filed, this dispute has divided public opinion, aggravated public concern about the growing number of Islamic minorities in France, and stirred up a hornet's nest of debate about religion and education. On paper, Ms. Matahout's case rests on how one defines a secular state and the extent to which personal expression, religious freedom, and an equal access to public employment intersect. Ms. Matahout maintains that the headscarf is a matter of personal preference and is neither a political statement nor an endorsement of Islam as a religion. State officials disagree. They maintain that the scarf is a religious symbol, one that violates the neutral position of schools in regard to religious beliefs. Other opponents of Ms. Matahout's right to wear a scarf while teaching maintain that the scarf is a device of social control in Islamic cultures, a means to repress women and constrict their freedom of movement.

Ms. Matahout's supporters argue that she is an unlikely supporter for oppression of women. The daughter of a diplomat who has been exposed to a number of different Arab and Western cultures, Ms. Matahout surprised her own family by donning the headscarf in 2001. They have commented that Ms. Matahout described her decision as an expression of identity and a matter of personal faith.

As the matter stands, when the high court meets to decide her case later this month, their decision may have more to do with the separation of church and state than with freedom of expression.

Passport

● ●

● PURPOSE

- To focus groups on the importance of knowledge sharing as a means of team building.

- To demonstrate to individuals the importance of sharing information about their professional skills, talents, and significant experiences.

● GAME OBJECTIVE

To be the first team that completes its passports.

● PLAYERS

Eight or more.

● TIME

Forty to sixty minutes.

● SUPPLIES

- One "passport" for each player.

- One set of twenty sticker dots for each team; each team should be assigned a different color—red, yellow, blue, and green.

- Four sticker dots (one each red, yellow, blue, and green) for each player.

- An overhead projector (if using transparencies) or a newsprint flip chart and felt-tipped markers.

- Felt-tipped markers for each team to decorate passport covers.

- Pens for each team, to fill in passport information.

● PREPARATION

Create one "passport" for each player by folding three standard 8 1/2-inch × 11-inch sheets in half and then stapling the folded sheets of paper along the spine.

The passport should consist of four internal pages. Only the front side of each page will be used during the game.

● GAME PLAY

1. Divide the group into four teams and assign each team one corner of the room.

2. Inform participants that they will create personal "passports" that contain information of the professional and personal skills, talents, and experience they bring to their teams.

3. Give a brief overview of the game:

   "The object of the game is for each player to receive four dots—one dot for each page of the passport.

   "To receive a dot, each player must present his or her credentials to all four teams—his or her own team and the other three teams. When the credential is 'approved' by a member of the awarding blue, green, red, or yellow team, the team member awards a colored dot representing a 'stamp of approval' of that team.

   "Your first task is to prepare your own passport."

4. Distribute one passport and one set of four dots (blue, green, red, or yellow) to each player.

5. Give participants 10 minutes to create their "passports."

6. Tell them to write "Passport" in large letters on the cover. Write their profession, function, or discipline, such as Systems Analyst, Operations Engineer, Training Specialist, or Plant Foreman (substitute a department or geographic location, if necessary). Write their full name and any nicknames by which they prefer to be known.

7. Have them number each interior page 1 through 4 (use only the front side of each page—the reverse should stay blank).

   - On Page 1 . . .

     Place the Blue dot on top of page.

     Enter "academic and professional credentials," such as: holds Microsoft certification, earned associate's degree in web design, published article in professional trade journal.

   - On Page 2 . . .

     Place the Green dot on top of the page.

     Enter "individual talents, knacks, or gifts" such as: works well with numbers, considered a good negotiator, plays a musical instrument, sings in a chorus or choir, good woodworking skills.

   - On Page 3 . . .

     Place the Red dot on top of the page.

     Enter "workplace experience and credentials," such as: company veteran, someone who "gets things done," accident free for five years, excellent attendance record, was salesperson of the week.

   - On Page 4 . . .

     Place the Yellow dot on top of the page.

     Enter "personality characteristics that make me a good person to know," such as: good sense of humor, good listener, good problem solver, creative, reliable.

8. Call time after 10 minutes.

9. Designate each team a color—red, blue, green, or yellow—and then give each team twenty colored dots that correspond to their team color.

Each team now represents one page of the passport.

- Only members of the Blue team can award a blue dot for page 1.

- Only members of the Green team can award a green dot for page 2.

- Only members of the Red team can award a red dot for page 3.

- Only members of the Yellow team can award a yellow dot for page 4.

10. Give each team 5 minutes to plan strategy and to award dots to its own members.

11. Call time after 5 minutes.

12. Introduce the game:

    "Each player now has 20 minutes to complete his or her credentialing—that is, he or she must receive one dot for each of the four pages. Since you already have your own team's dot, you should concentrate on getting a dot from a member of the other three teams.

    "The first team in which all members have completed their passports wins."

13. Players seek the three other teams to fill their passports with colored dots.

14. When all members of a single team are credentialed, they should notify the facilitator.

15. Call time at the end of 20 minutes or if all players have completed their passports.

    The first team whose members complete their passports win.

● POST-GAME DEBRIEFING

The central task of this exercise is for group members to get to know each other in significant, rather than trivial ways. How they go about doing that (and how long they take to do it) is what you will be processing with the group. Ask:

- Beyond filling out your passport, what did your team learn as a result of this exercise?

- How long does it normally take in our organization to accumulate this much information about each other?

- What makes it easier (or more difficult) to get to know others on our team?

- What's the value of having this kind of information all in one place?

- What incentives are there to share information about ourselves in our organization?

- What does the organization do (if anything) to make it easy to find people according to their credentials, expertise, or talents?

- What strategies do you use to make yourself known in an organization?

- What additional information could the Passport carriers have asked that would have helped you play to the strengths of other team members?

- As you went through this exercise did you or any of your team members experience any reluctance about sharing your credentials or acknowledging your accomplishments?

- Is this reluctance to "toot our own horn" a problem in our organization?

● GENERAL COMMENTS

- This may seem a complicated way to introduce players to each other. But once you have experienced the high energy and "sharing" that occurs during this event, it will become a staple of your training regimen. Players enjoy the opportunity to develop and present themselves to their peers. And the level of information and feedback is extremely high during the play and debriefing of this game. This game is an excellent way for intact work teams to get to know one another and is especially helpful before starting a special project. It also serves to underscore that all of us are citizens or members of numerous groups—our families, our communities, and our organizations. In each of these settings we present ourselves for approval and acceptance. Our ability to describe persuasively and effectively the value we bring is an important skill.

- The "passport" to team acceptance is our ability to demonstrate potential value-added to our would-be colleagues. People need to know what we can bring to the team that will help them succeed. By the design of the game, participants are STRONGLY ENCOURAGED to share their *most significant* credentials, talents, experiences, and characteristics.

- In addition to the suggested credentials for academic or professional experience, individual talents, significant work experience, or personal characteristics, there are alternate "credentials" you may want to include in the passport, including—languages spoken, point of national or cultural origin, number of countries visited, or some other aspect of experience that is interesting or useful.

- There are many ways groups may approach this task. Other than getting the dots on the correct pages with a legible (and coherent) explanation of why the dot was awarded, there are no rules to be kept or broken.

- *Partner Up.* A processing point is whether or not two or more players choose to "partner up" in representing each other and gathering dots. The way this commonly works is that one person will act as the "agent" for another, representing his or her accomplishments in the most splendid and favorable light. Because they have no inhibitions about representing someone else, they may end up garnering more dots for each other than they would have by each acting on their own behalf.

- To compute the required number of dots, simply double the dot count (in each color) for every player—one dot to mark each page and one dot received from each team.

● CUSTOMIZING PASSPORT

Size of Group

- For groups of six to ten, play as two teams.

- For larger groups of twenty-five to fifty, play as instructed, but allow more time for players to collect their dots.

Time of Play

- Shorten or lengthen the time allowed for collecting dots.

Method of Play

- Have the awarding player sign or otherwise "personalize" the dot to designate approval as well as to distinguish the dot from the page marker. (A player receives a red dot, signed by a member of the Red team and then places the dot on the appropriate page, also marked with a red dot.)

- Change the credentials required to meet the needs and focus of your specific team or organization.

- Have players form groups of two's and three's in their quest for dots. (See "Partner Up" in the General Comments section.)

Scoring

- Award 1 point for each dot received. The team with the most points wins.

- Award a bonus of 10 points for each passport completed.

Passport

- Divide into four teams—each team is designated a color.

- Meet in appropriate corners.

- Prepare your "passport."

- Each team receives twenty team-colored dots.

- Complete your passport by collecting one dot from each team for your credentials in each of the four areas.

- The first team to complete all their passports wins.

Proxy*

● ●

● **PURPOSE**

   • To explore the elements of effective delegation.

● **GAME OBJECTIVE**

   To collect as many points as possible.

● **PLAYERS**

   Eight or more.

● **TIME**

   Thirty-five to sixty minutes.

● **SUPPLIES**

   • One set of four Proxy cards for each team.

   • One set of fifteen topic questions in various topics, prepared in advance by the facilitator. The questions can be on separate cards or on one page of paper.

---

*Proxy was suggested by the "A, B, or C Card" interactive exercise used by Karen Lawson at the ASTD International Conference. Thanks, Karen.

- One set of six Response Sheets for each team.
- Several felt-tipped markers to prepare the Proxy cards.
- Stopwatch and call bell.

● PREPARATION

Prepare one set of Proxy cards for each team by selecting index cards in four colors, such as green, red, blue, and yellow. Using a felt-tipped marker, write "Leader" and then "A," "B," and "C" (for players A, B, and C) on the blank sides of each of the four cards. The different color cards allows the facilitator to easily identify who is responsible for responding to a question.

Prepare one set of six Response Sheets for each team by photocopying the page containing six Response Sheets (at the back of the game), cutting each page into six separate sheets, and then stapling the six sheets into a set.

● GAME PLAY

1. Divide the group into teams of four players.

2. Distribute one set of Proxy cards to each team.

3. Have each team select a leader.

4. Have the team leader keep the "Leader" card and then distribute one A, B, and C card to each team member.

5. Distribute one set of Response Sheets to each team.

6. Announce or post the topic areas from which the set of questions will be drawn.

7. Have teams meet for 3 minutes to determine topic responsibility areas.

Round 1

1. Announce the topic of the first question.

2. Give each team leader 10 seconds to delegate the responsibility for responding to the question and to provide any instructions, as necessary.

3. Each team immediately informs the facilitator of the team proxy by holding up their Proxy card. Any team not showing its Proxy card is ineligible to play in that round.

4. Present the first question.

5. The proxy records the team's response on the Response Sheet.

6. Collect one Response Sheet from each team.

Scoring

1. If the response is correct, award 3 points.

2. If the response is incorrect, deduct 1 point.

3. If the team is ineligible, they receive 0 points.

Subsequent Play

1. Each round is played in a similar fashion.

2. Declare the team with the most points the winner.

● POST-GAME DEBRIEFING

The following questions will help groups explore what constitutes effective delegation:

- What did this experience reveal about the elements of effective delegation?

- If you were to create a "best practices for delegation" checklist for team leaders, what would you include?

- How are tasks normally assigned within your unit?

- What are the plusses and minuses of that approach to delegation?

- How should a manager or team leader test for talent in his or her group?

- What sort of support or information do you expect when someone appoints you the "proxy"?

- What responsibility (if any) did you feel toward the person who was appointed "proxy"?

● GENERAL COMMENTS

- Proxy allows you to simulate delegation in a pressure situation. This, in turn, allows your players to observe how they and their fellow team members acted during a stressful situation.

- By incorporating your own content or issues into the questions, you can reinforce learning and, at the same time, improve group understanding of how to delegate effectively. Delegating in any situation is affected by:

  - The level of group knowledge, experience, and ability.

  - Team leader understanding of and confidence in team member abilities.

- How well a leader delegates is determined by how well they are able to:

  - Match the task to team member talents.

  - Clarify expectations.

  - Provide whatever support is available.

  - Provide encouragement and coaching.

● SAMPLE PLAY

1. The group is divided into two teams—Team 1 and Team 2.

2. Each team is given a set of Proxy cards and Response Sheets.

3. Each team selects a leader.

4. The team leaders distribute the A, B, and C Proxy cards.

Round 1

1. The facilitator announces the first question topic: stress management.

2. Both team leaders make their assignments. Team 1's leader advises his proxy to "relax."

3. Both proxies hold up their cards to show who is the designated proxy.

   - Team 1's proxy is Player B.

   - Team 2's proxy is the team leader.

4. The question is presented: "What beverage is the most frequently consumed source of caffeine in the United States?"

5. Both proxy players write their responses down on their Response Sheets.

6. After 30 seconds the facilitator collects both sheets.

7. The correct response is presented: "Coffee."

   - Team 1 responded: "soft drinks."

   - Team 2 responded: "coffee."

8. The facilitator posts the points on the flip chart:

   - Team 1 = −1 point

   - Team 2 = +3 points

9. This ends play for Round 1.

Round 2

1. The facilitator announces the second question topic: customer service. Team 1's leader selects Frank from security, saying: "Remember your HR training."

2. Only Team 1's player holds up his Proxy card.

3. Team 1's proxy is Player A. Team 2 must sit out this round.

4. The question is presented: "Name the consumer protest technique that business people hate the most."

5. Team 1's proxy responds and the facilitator collects the Response Sheet.

6. The correct response is presented: "Picketing."

   - Team 1 responded: "Picketing."

7. The facilitator posts the points on the flip chart:

   - Team 1 = 3 points + −1 points [Round 1] = +2 points

   - Team 2 = 0 points +3 points [Round 1] = +3 points

8. This ends play for Round 2.

● CUSTOMIZING PROXY

Size of Group

- Divide smaller groups into one or two teams of four players each.

- Divide larger groups into multiple teams of four players. Allow for more time to handle the question topic and game administration.

Time of Play

- Shorten or lengthen the time for a round of play depending on the difficulty of the question material or the understanding level of the class.

- Expand or contract the number of rounds of play.

Method of Play

- Eliminate the Response Sheets by allowing for oral responses to each question. Play in the normal fashion—announce the topic and allow the team leader to select the proxy who writes down his or her response. Then have the proxy or team leader report the response to the facilitator.

- Create question sets that deal with topics appropriate to your audience.

- Create two or more levels of difficulty for each question. Use the "easier" questions in the beginning of play to allow players to get used to the rules and roles. Use the more challenging questions after the third round.

Scoring

- Change the scoring for incorrect responses to minus 3 points. This will increase pressure on the team leader.

Proxy

· ·

- **Form teams of four players:**

    One team leader

    Three players (A, B, C)

- **After topic areas are announced, hold a brief team meeting to determine who will be responsible for which topic.**

- **First topic is announced.**

- **Team leader has 10 seconds to assign response to self or player A, B, or C.**

- **Responding player shows Proxy card.**

- **Question is presented.**

- **Scoring:**

    If response is correct, award 3 points.

    If incorrect, deduct 1 point.

- **All rounds are played the same.**

RESPONSE SHEET FOR PROXY

Team _____

Round _____

Response _____

_____

RESPONSE SHEET FOR PROXY

Team _____

Round _____

Response _____

_____

RESPONSE SHEET FOR PROXY

Team _____

Round _____

Response _____

_____

RESPONSE SHEET FOR PROXY

Team _____

Round _____

Response _____

_____

RESPONSE SHEET FOR PROXY

Team _____

Round _____

Response _____

_____

RESPONSE SHEET FOR PROXY

Team _____

Round _____

Response _____

_____

Rear View Mirror

. . . .

● **PURPOSE**

- To demonstrate the importance of team trust and communication.

- To demonstrate and practice one-on-one coaching skills.

- To demonstrate the dynamics of "walking the talk."

● **GAME OBJECTIVE**

To safely cross the Obstacle Grid in the shortest time.

● **PLAYERS**

Six or more.

● **TIME**

Thirty-five to fifty-five minutes.

● **SUPPLIES**

- One or more rolls of masking tape.

- Overhead projector (if using transparencies) or a newsprint flip chart and felt-tipped markers.

- One Obstacle Grid Sheet for each team.

- Noisemaker (optional).

- Stopwatch or timer (optional).

● PREPARATION

Create a floor grid (four-by-four Tic-Tac-Toe grid) as follows:

- Using masking tape, outline a six-foot square on the floor.

- Divide the square into four sections by placing three six-foot strips of tape vertically.

- Complete the sixteen 18-inch squares by placing three six-foot strips of tape horizontally.

Prepare one Obstacle Grid Sheet for each team. (See Obstacle Grids at the end of this game.)

● GAME PLAY

1. Divide the group into two to four teams.

2. Have each team select one floorwalker—it is the "walker's" task to safely walk backwards through the obstacle course.

3. Have each team select a coach—it is the coach's task to talk or guide the walker safely through the grid.

4. Explain the following rules:

   - The coach may not touch the walker.

   - The coach issues a set of verbal instructions to the walker.

   - The walker cannot talk with the coach.

   - The walker must cross within the grid by using diagonal or side or back moves.

   - The walker may move only one square at a time—jumping over squares is not allowed.

Round 1

1. Distribute one Obstacle Grid to the first coach.

2. While the coach is familiarizing himself or herself with the grid, have the walker step to the front of the floor grid.

3. When the coach approaches the grid, have the walker face away from the grid—that is, the walker should be in front of the grid so that any steps he or she takes are backwards and onto the grid. The coach should be facing the walker.

4. Without touching the walker, the coach has 1 minute to verbally guide the walker through the grid.

5. If the walker steps on an obstacle square, the team must start over.

6. Call time at the end of 1 minute or when the walker safely transverses the grid.

7. Play is the same for all rounds.

● POST-GAME DEBRIEFING

In life we may have some say in the choice of our coach. But typically, we are assigned a coach, if we have a coach at all.

   - If we were able to choose one however, what qualities would we look for in a coach?

- What specifically would we like him or her to do so that the coaching would be of greatest help to us?

Once the exercise is complete, ask the walkers, whose job was to "walk the talk":

- What is the most useful feedback you received?

- What happened when you got contradictory advice?

- Did the quality of coaching or feedback you received improve over time? What changed?

- If you were to "coach your coach" what would you have him or her do differently in leading you through the grid?

Ask the coaches, whose job was to "talk the walk":

- What were the challenges you faced in trying to help others?

- How did you go about trying to find out what the walker needed?

- How did you explain the task to yourself before you tried to explain it to someone else?

- Were you open or resistant to the idea of anyone else providing feedback or coaching?

- What did you do as a result?

● GENERAL COMMENTS

- We all know that it's harder to back up than it is to drive forward. Yet it's a cliché of history that military planners seem to prepare to fight the last war. Similarly, some people in the workplace are so focused on what has been that they appear to drive by looking in their rear view mirrors. Rear View Mirror turns the planning process on its head by asking teams to figure out how to communicate with each other in order to proceed backwards.

- Rear View Mirror is a very "hands on," physical demonstration of the importance of good coaching and timely feedback—talking the walk—in order to figure out initially what we are supposed to do and then to improve our performance over time. In this exercise participants must rely on coaching and feedback in order to move at all because the maneuvers they must follow are literally out of sight behind them.

- Rear View Mirror presents rich opportunities to discuss what it is like when we are expected to work "in the dark," "wearing blinders," or with an inadequate vision of where we need to go. Like any novice worker, participants cannot foresee all the things they must do in order to complete the assigned task. The only one who can help them succeed is their coach. The first time any of us attempts a new task we need to rely on coaching and feedback from others to understand what is needed and how best to accomplish it. This game clearly demonstrates the importance of coaching to help both individuals and teams succeed.

- In setting up this game, take a few minutes up-front to engage the group in discussing how we find out what we are supposed to be doing. Probable responses include:

  Read the regulations.

  Take a class.

  Do what the boss tells you.

  Observe what others do.

  Figure it out on your own.

  Have your teammates explain what to do.

- A common denominator of successful performance—whatever the source of instruction—is that once you start doing a thing, it helps to have someone who is ready, willing, and able to point out what you are doing right, what you are doing wrong, and where you might improve. Without feedback, all of us are literally "blind." Explain that, in this exercise, the point is to discover just how critical it is to be able to ask for and receive timely, specific, helpful feedback on what needs to happen and how you are doing as you go along.

- If you see that your coaches seem "stuck," call a time out and inquire whether the coaches have established a reference for the Obstacle Grid to help them with the walk. Introduce this simple grid pattern to help your coaches "talk the walk."

1	2	3	4
5	6	7	8
9	10	11	12
13	14	15	16

● SAMPLE PLAY

1. Group is divided into two sets of five-player teams.

2. Team A selects a walker, who is led to the start position.

3. Team A's coach receives an Obstacle Grid, as shown below:

Starting Position

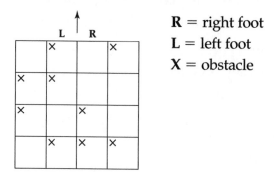

R = right foot
L = left foot
X = obstacle

4. The coach directs walker to place her right foot back into the first open square.*

5. The coach then directs walker to place her left foot into same square.

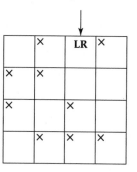

6. The coach directs the walker to place her right foot behind her left foot.

7. The coach then directs the walker to place her left foot back into the same square.

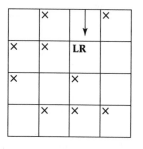

*All obstructed squares are marked with an "x."

8. The coach directs the walker to place her left foot diagonally back one square.

9. The coach then directs the walker to place her right foot back into the same square.

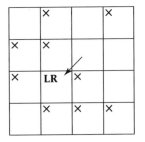

10. The coach directs the walker to place her left foot diagonally back one square.

11. The coach then directs the walker to place her right foot back into the same square.

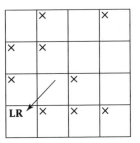

12. The coach directs the walker to step off of the grid, left foot back one square.

13. The coach then directs walker to place her right foot next to her left foot.

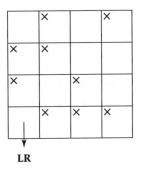

14. Team A has successfully walked through the Obstacle Grid.

15. The facilitator notes that it took 53 seconds and posts "53" on the flip chart easel.

● CUSTOMIZING REAR VIEW MIRROR

Size of Group

- For groups six or fewer, play as one team.

- For larger groups:

  - Play separate rounds of one team completing the grid while other players observe. Each new round should consist of a different Obstacle Grid. When teams observe others in play, they have a greater appreciation for the communication procedures required in the walk.

  - Conduct simultaneous exercises on multiple grids. Playing multiple grids may increase competition.

Time of Play

- Shorten the time to 30 seconds or lengthen the time to 2 or 3 minutes, depending on the difficulty of the Obstacle Grid or the skill of the audience.

Method of Play

- If the walker steps on an obstacle square, that team is eliminated.

- Allow the walker to converse with his or her coach before and during the grid maneuver.

- Select a team of walkers and have the coaches guide the walkers through one Obstacle Grid. Then have the walker and coach trade roles to see how they would perform in the other role.

- Play background music that may assist or even detract from the grid maneuver. Debrief the distracting music as players getting cues from two different and sometimes conflicting sources.

- Have walker select his or her own personal coach.

- Have coach select his or her own personal walker.

- Create an "impasse," where walker is blocked in by obstacles. Observe how the coach attempts to deal with the obstacle—shut down, negotiate a change, or make his or her own rules, such as stepping off and then onto the grid to get around the obstacle.

Scoring

- Award 25 points to each team that successfully crosses the grid within the prescribed time.

- Award 25 points for the most "creative" crossing moves.

- Award 1 bonus point for each second that a team crosses the grid under the allowed time.

- **Divide the group into two to four teams.**

- **Select one coach and one walker.**

- **Walker stands in front of the floor grid, facing the coach.**

- **Coach verbally guides the walker to safely go backwards through the obstacle in less than 1 minute.**

- **The team that crosses the grid in the shortest time wins.**

OBSTACLE GRID #1 FOR
Rear View Mirror

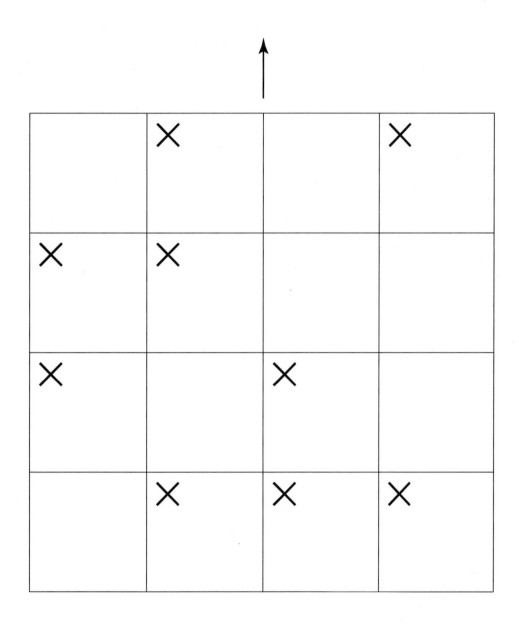

OBSTACLE GRID #2 FOR
Rear View Mirror

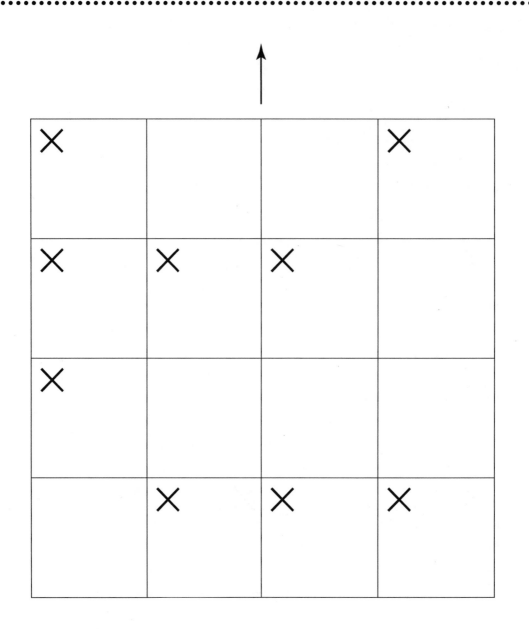

OBSTACLE GRID #3 FOR
Rear View Mirror

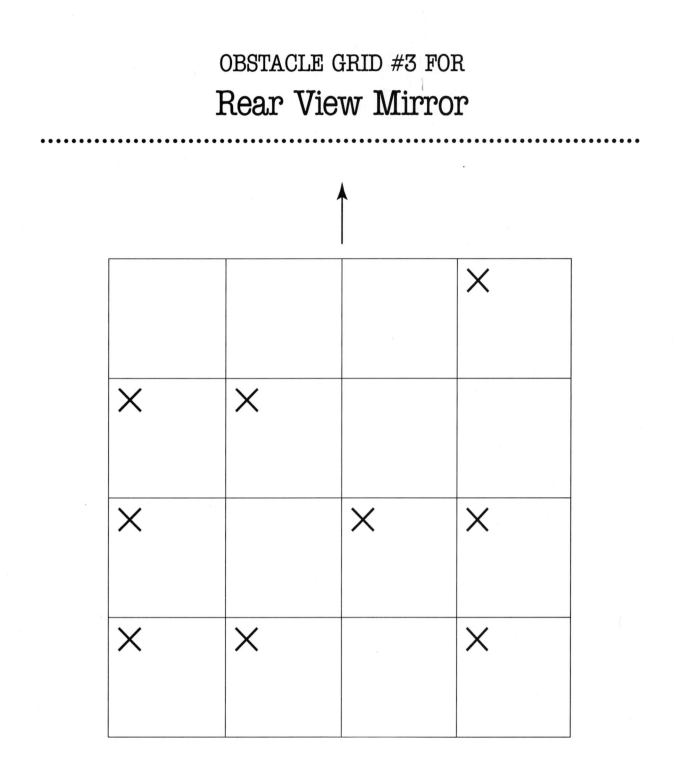

OBSTACLE GRID #4 FOR
Rear View Mirror

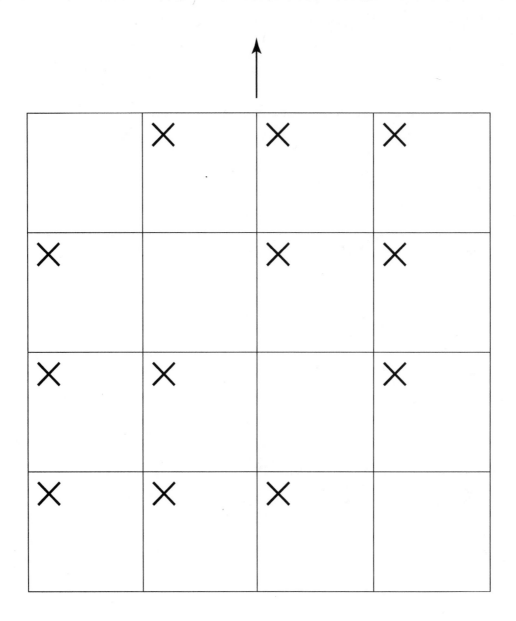

OBSTACLE GRID #5 FOR
Rear View Mirror

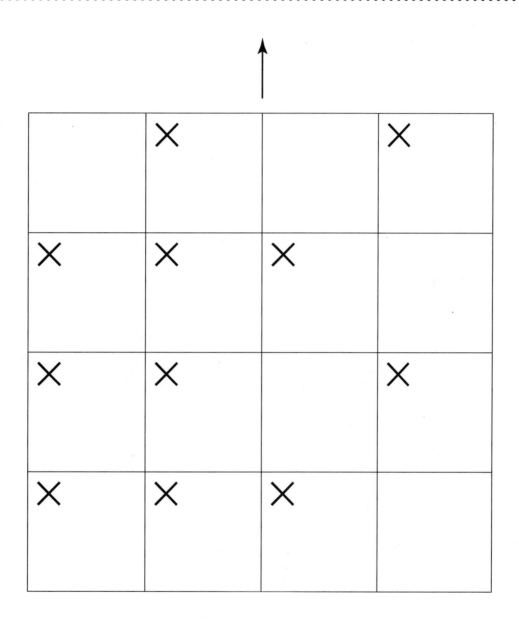

OBSTACLE GRID #6 (IMPASSE!) FOR
Rear View Mirror

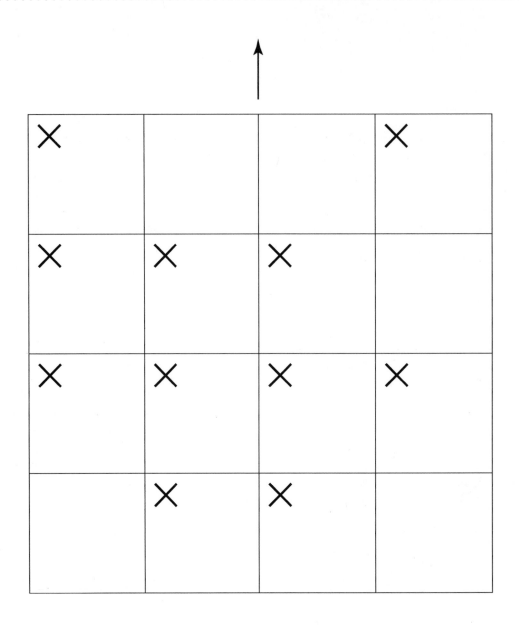

Sandwiches

● PURPOSE

- To show how brainstorming can be used to expand the range of possible solutions.
- To warm up a group prior to problem solving.

● GAME OBJECTIVE

To score the most team points.

● PLAYERS

Nine to thirty.

● TIME

Twenty to sixty minutes.

● SUPPLIES

- Paper and pens or pencils for each team.
- Flip chart and set of felt-tipped markers.

- An overhead projector (if using transparencies).

- Masking tape (optional).

- Stopwatch or timing device.

● GAME PLAY

1. Divide the group into teams of three to five players.

2. Have each team sit at its own table.

3. Distribute paper and pens or pencils to each team.

4. Have each team select a team name.

5. Explain that you will provide each team with a mini-word and that the teams will then have 5 minutes to create as many word "sandwiches"—words using the mini-word as a prefix, suffix, or sandwiched in the word—as possible.

6. Say that to qualify, all "sandwich" words must be found in a standard dictionary.

7. Present the following example: Using the mini-word "out" . . .

   Prefix = outward, outrageous

   Suffix = lockout, about

   Sandwich = southern, couture

8. Ask all teams to write their team names on their papers.

Round 1

1. Post the new mini-word on a flip chart or overhead transparency.

2. Inform the teams that they have 5 minutes to write as many "sandwiches" as they can on the pieces of paper.

3. Call time after 5 minutes.

4. Collect the pieces of paper from each team.

5. Award 2 points for each word created by the team. Award a 5-point bonus for an "orphan" word, any word NOT listed on any other team's sheet.

6. All rounds are played the same. Post a new mini-word and have teams create as many "sandwiches" as they can in 5 minutes.

7. Make sure each team has a blank sheet of paper on which to write for each round.

8. Declare the team with the most points the winner.

● SAMPLE PLAY

1. Class is divided into two teams, Team A and Team B.

2. Each team is given paper and pens or pencils.

3. Each team selects and writes its name on the paper.

Round 1

1. The mini-word "ant" is written on the newsprint easel.

2. Give teams 5 minutes to list as many "ants" as possible.

3. After 5 minutes, the facilitator calls time and collects a list from each team.

Review of the Word Lists

1. Team A created twenty-one words:

Prefix—anteater, antelope, antenna, antic, anticipation, antifreeze, antipasto, antiseptic, antisubmarine, antlers, anthrax

Suffix—buoyant, giant, instant, pant, vibrant, want

Sandwiches—frantic, mantle, panther, wanton

2. Team B created twenty-two words:

Prefix—antacid, Antarctica, antenna, anterior, anthem, antichrist, anticipation, antifreeze, antipasto, antique, antiseptic, antlers, anthrax

Suffix—buoyant, giant, vibrant

Sandwiches—gigantic, mantle, panther, pants, unwanted, wanted

(Another way to check the list for words and orphans is to have each team create a list of its words on a piece of newsprint. A volunteer then reads his or her team's word list and the other team marks through any duplicates on its list; when there are no duplicates, the word is identified as an "orphan," and scored accordingly.)

Scoring

- Team A scoring:

  21 words @ 2 points per word; total = 42 points

  7 orphan words @ 5 points per word; total = 35 points (anteater, antelope, antic, antisubmarine, frantic, instant, wanton)

  77 points

- Team B scoring:

  22 words @ 2 points per word, total = 44 points

  8 orphan words @ 5 points per word, total = 40 points (antacid, Antarctica, anterior, anthem, antichrist, antique, gigantic, unwanted)

  84 points

- Team B wins the round.

● POST-GAME DEBRIEFING

Writing the "ant" creates an implied limit—that only a creature with feelers and six legs qualifies. In fact "ant" is contained in each of the sandwich words provided in sample play. It is generally the case that we begin problem solving with a strongly implied set of limits.

After Round One, ask each team:

- Which "ants" did you identify first?

- Who was the first to break free of the insect "ant"?

- Did you do any categorization of ideas once you generated them?

- What was the reaction of the team?

- Did one idea by one person lead to another idea by someone else?

- As you went through Round One, what assumptions did you find about what constituted a "right" answer?

After Round Two, ask each team:

- What was different in this round than the way you approached Round One?

- Did you attempt any division of labor (for example, a couple of people thinking of words beginning with ant and some focusing on endings with ant), or did you continue with everyone simply contributing whatever words they thought of?

- Did you change anything about how you captured ideas?

- Did you change anything that enabled you to generate a larger volume of ideas?

- Did you reject any ideas?

● GENERAL COMMENTS

- Think of the word "sandwich" as fitting between the letter (regular sandwich) and going before or after the other letters (open-faced sandwich). This exercise underscores the different paths that participants take to solve problems.

- Creativity is not simply a matter of coming up with a new idea; it also involves thinking about old ideas in new applications. Sandwiches demonstrates the power of simply focusing on generating a volume of ideas before exercising judgment about which are acceptable, right, or wrong.

- The instructions place no constraints whatsoever on players. By listening to each other's lists of "ants," it quickly becomes obvious that there are many ways to approach this task and a wide range of completely acceptable answers. The concept of Sandwiches fits our work philosophy of adapting and using the best available combinations of material and human resources.

For example:

- Players may categorize "ant" not only as a particular kind of insect (fire ant, army ant, red ant) but also in terms of:

  Animals: elephant, antelope, panther

  Geographic Place Names: Santa Barbara, Canterbury, Antipodes

  Proper Names: Emanuel Kant, Antigone, Santa Claus, Cantinflas, Marie Antoinette

---

Nouns: cantaloupe, lieutenant, pantomime

Adjectives: dilettante, antiquated, intolerant

Medical Terms: antiseptic, anthrax, antibodies

Religious Terms: supplicant, communicant, celebrant, tantric

Foreign Words: tante (French for aunt), mantilla (Spanish for lace head scarf), cantina (Spanish for bar or pub)

- Players can think of "ant" in terms of the position where it appears in a word:

Prefix: antipasto, antic, antique

Suffix: operant, synchophant, militant

Sandwich: phantom, philanthropist, plantation

● CUSTOMIZING SANDWICHES

Size of Group

- For smaller groups of six to ten players, divide the group into two teams.

- For larger-sized groups divide into four or five teams. Have one team read its list aloud and have other groups cross through any repeated words. Have each team tally its score, which is then posted by the facilitator.

Time of Play

- Shorten the time of play for larger groups to allow for team presentations and scoring.

- Lengthen the time for more difficult mini-words.

Method of Play

- Allow teams to share information to reinforce cooperative learning.

- Allow teams to "purchase" the use of a dictionary for 25 points. This can be used to weigh the costs against advantages of learning technologies. Reinforce this during scoring by subtracting the 25 points and then comparing the "bare" score against other scores.

- Allow only one team to purchase the use of a dictionary. This will introduce topics of ethics in team play or the competitive approach of "winning at all costs."

- Allow teams to use foreign words and phrases, geographic references, trade vernacular, and proper names.

Scoring

- Increase the bonuses for "orphan" words to encourage creativity over quantity.

- Award a special 15-point bonus for the most unique or creative word.

Sandwiches

· ·

- **Form into teams of three to five players.**

- **Facilitator will introduce the "mini-word."**

- **Take 5 minutes to create as many word sandwiches using the mini-word as possible.**

- **Scoring: Your team receives:**

   2 points for each word.

   5 points for each orphan (unique) word.

- **The team with the most points wins.**

Scavenger Bingo

PURPOSE

- To serve as a lively icebreaker in introducing new team members while kicking off group work.

- To spur lateral thinking and to uncover problem-solving talents within the team.

GAME OBJECTIVE

To win by covering the required Game Sheet spaces.

PLAYERS

Twelve or more.

TIME

Fifteen to forty-five minutes.

SUPPLIES

- One Game Sheet per team.

- One Item Checklist per team.

- An overhead projector (if using transparencies) or a newsprint flip chart and felt-tipped markers.

- Pens or pencils for each team.

● GAME PLAY

1. Divide the group into teams of four or more players each.

2. Distribute one Game Sheet, one Item Checklist, and pens or pencils to each team.

3. Instruct the teams to locate items suggested by the clues in each space.

4. Tell teams that when they find an item to record it on their Item Checklist and then cover the appropriate space on the Game Sheet by making an "X" through that space.

5. The task is complete when a team covers a complete row either horizontally, vertically, or diagonally. (For additional patterns see Alternate Versions for Scavenger Bingo at the end of the game.)

5. Declare the first team to cover the required spaces the winner.

● POST-GAME DEBRIEFING

To highlight the impact of assumptions and shared definitions on team performance, select some of the following questions when debriefing this game:

- Who took the initiative on your team to clarify the rules so that you were all proceeding from a shared understanding of what you were to do?

- Who suggested that there might be multiple interpretations of each Bingo requirement? For example, "half dollar" could be satisfied with two quarters, five dimes, fifty cents, the letters "dol" or "lar" written on a sheet of paper ("dol" is half of the word dollar), or a dollar folded in half.

- Did you follow up on the possibility of multiple interpretations to surface other assumptions about the game? If so, what assumptions did you identify?

- Did anyone protest if he or she felt that the rules were being "broken"? What happened as a result?

- Which definition or interpretation of a Bingo requirement provoked the most discussion?

- Was there any division of labor on your team? In other words, did you assign specific requirements to specific people, or did you all work together to satisfy all requirements?

- What were the benefits (if any) to a division of labor?

- What were the benefits (if any) to working collaboratively on all requirements?

- What did you learn about your colleagues—what they know, their experience, or how they think—as a result of this game?

● GENERAL COMMENTS

- This game turbo charges teams by throwing them directly into a performance challenge with little time to "form, storm, or norm." Teams win based on how quickly they can combine a Bingo strategy with imaginative problem solving. How they interpret the scavenger requirements will strongly affect their strategy. Discussing their interpretations is a powerful way to show the importance of unstated assumptions on group performance.

- Scavenger Bingo is also an excellent "meet and cooperate" game for groups seated at conference tables, for newly formed teams who do not yet know each other well, and for teams of six or more—usually considered too unwieldy for other games.

- There are many ways to satisfy the requirements of any specific Bingo square. For example, in addition to "half dollar," as discussed in the debriefing, a "K" item could be any object beginning with "K" or "OK" or any object belonging to a person named Kay; a "pie" item could be a "pie chart"; something musical could be "two spoons"; and so on.

- To discourage simultaneous Bingos, create Game Sheets with differing patterns of clues. This can be done manually (four or five configurations) or by using "Zingo," a computer program that randomly sorts and prints your Game Sheets (www.thiagi.com).

● CUSTOMIZING SCAVENGER BINGO

Size of Group

- For smaller groups of six or fewer, form one team and distribute one Game Sheet.

- For larger groups, use several Game Sheets. Alter the Game Sheets by either changing the configurations of the clues or by requiring differing patterns of solution of the Game Sheet (one team fills the outer frame, another team fills a crossing pattern, etc.).

Time of Play

- Shorten the time by decreasing the number of spaces to be covered (four or five in a row).

- Lengthen time requirements by increasing the requirement to more elaborate configurations (outside frame, "blackout" or complete frame).

Method of Play

- Create your own variation of the five-by-five grid with clues specific to your audience.

- Create a variety of grid patterns, including customized "letters" for your group. The patterns include:

  - Big "O" or Outside Frame.

  - Picture in a Frame or Inside Frame.

  - Blackout (all spaces).

  - Six-Pack (any set of squares that are two by three).

  - Letters: H, I, L, N, O, S, T, U, X, Z.

  (See the Alternate Versions for Scavenger Bingo at the end of this game.)

- Create special clues that lead teams to seek out items found in your training room.

- Write clues in different languages that might be familiar to certain players. See if this encourages sharing among teams.

- Write clues in special technical or trade jargon, such as chemical formulae (NaCl) or jargon codes (F2F), to challenge your players.

- Write clues based on company-based nomenclature or culture.

- Challenge your players' creativity with ambiguous decals—☺—to see how they interpret and solve the clue.

- To create easier play, put a "free space" on each Game Sheet.

Scoring

- Award 25 points for each team that successfully completes the assignment.

- Award a bonus of 10 points for the first team to successfully complete the assignment.

- If the time of play expires with no winners, declare the team with the MOST spaces covered as the winner.

Scavenger Bingo

....

- Form teams of four or more players.

- Each team receives an Item Checklist and a Game Sheet.

- Mark an "X" through the required spaces on the Game Sheet when you have met the criteria for that space.

- The first team to complete the required pattern of spaces wins.

GAME SHEET FOR
Scavenger Bingo

half dollar	something orange	something borrowed	power source	government form
First Aid item	something "ant"	"K" item	something magnetic	child's play
calendar	something musical	something woodsy	light source	something toxic
animal hair	something presidential	something chloride	something notched	something "clubby"
square cloth	baseball item	type of pie	something Italian	news-worthy

ITEM CHECKLIST FOR
Scavenger Bingo

Item Required	Item Tendered	How This Item Meets the Requirement

ALTERNATE VERSIONS FOR
Scavenger Bingo

#1: "X"

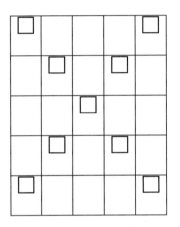

#2: Six Pack

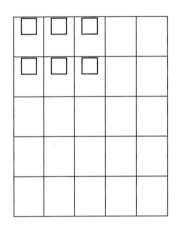

#3: Picture in the Frame
or Inside Frame

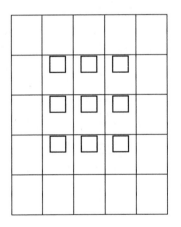

#4: "O" or Outside
Frame

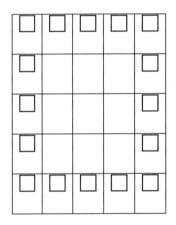

ALTERNATE VERSIONS FOR
Scavenger Bingo

. . . .

#5: "L"

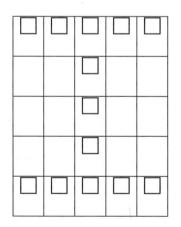

#6: "N"

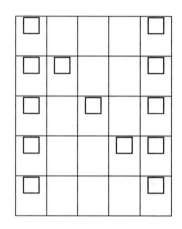

#7: "I"

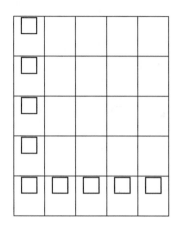

#8: "H" or Goalpost

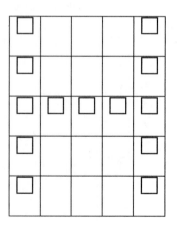

ALTERNATE VERSIONS FOR
Scavenger Bingo

#9: "U"

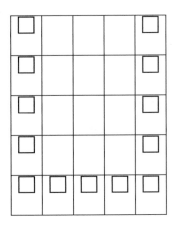

#10: "T"

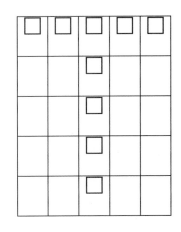

#11: "Z"

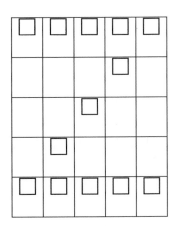

#12: "S"

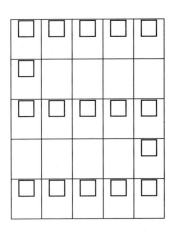

Second Mouse Gets the Cheese

. . . .

● PURPOSE

- To reinforce understanding of data and information.

- To practice estimation skills.

- To create a dialog about personal and corporate credibility.

● GAME OBJECTIVE

To score the most points.

● PLAYERS

Six or more.

● TIME

Twenty-five to sixty minutes.

● SUPPLIES

- One sheet of flip chart paper, masking tape, and felt-tipped markers.

- Seven or more problems, case studies, or questions on the topic, prepared in advance by the facilitator.

- An overhead projector (if using transparencies) or a newsprint flip chart and felt-tipped markers.

- Paper and pencils for each player.

- Set of index cards, two for each team, per round.

● GAME PLAY

1. Divide group into two to four teams.

2. Ask each team to select a team name.

3. Distribute a set of index cards and pens or pencils to each team.

4. Have teams write their team names on all of their cards.

Round 1

1. Present the first question.

2. Have each team write its response to the question on the index card.

3. Have teams place their "response" index cards face down on their tables.

4. On a second index card have each team predict which opponent(s) got the correct response and which opponent(s) got an incorrect response.

5. Have teams place their "prediction" index cards down on the table.

6. Collect both cards from each team.

7. Go over the correct response.

8. Scoring: For each team's . . .

   - *Correct response,* they receive 11 points.

   - *Correct prediction,* they receive 3 points.

9. This completes play for round one.

10. Play continues as in the first round.

11. Declare the team with the most points the winner.

● POST-GAME DEBRIEFING

The following questions will be helpful as you debrief the experience:

- How did you go about assessing whether or not the other team had guessed correctly? On what did you base your estimate?

- If their answers proved to be right, how did this change your assessment of their credibility?

- Within your organization who (either people or groups) has a good reputation for credibility? On what is that credibility based?

- Are there people in your organization who generally turn out to be right, but who lack credibility or voice? What is going on there?

- How can individuals and teams boost their credibility in the workplace? How do you assess whether or not other teams really "know their stuff"?

- How do we develop confidence that we "really know our stuff"?

- If you were unsure of your answer, did you try to bluff anyway?

- What are the consequences of bluffing in the workplace and in the team?

● GENERAL COMMENTS

- Some popular TV game shows, such as *Hollywood Squares,* are based on "secondary" responses—guessing the quality of a partner's response. This passion for "people watching" is reflected in Second Mouse Gets the Cheese.

- Robert Abrams, in *Game Theory,* proposed that players not only calculate their own play but also the likely play of their opponents. Thus, the most spirited play of the game may not be in your own response, but in predicting your opponent's responses.

- Second Mouse Gets the Cheese brings home the importance of creating a reputation for credibility within an organization. In any organization it is sometimes a matter of how confident you are about what you know (or clarity about what it is that you don't know) that counts for more than the knowledge itself.

- This game points up the impact that credibility can have on teams. It can also be used to illustrate the elements that go into creating credibility for individuals, for units, for groups, and for departments. We establish our credibility not only by being proven right by events, but by being able to establish our rationale, by being able to put facts and events in context, and by speaking confidently as to how it is that we know something. Tone of voice, a matter-of-fact delivery, and eye contact all contribute to the impression of confidence.

- In processing this exercise, elicit examples of people who—it later turned out—were dead right, but who were not believed because they lacked organizational credibility. Springboard into a discussion of how both teams and individuals can build their credibility.

- In this game, you are never "out of the loop," despite your own knowledge of the topic. Each team's intuition or observations can earn points. This brings another dimension to play . . . "play acting."

- Determine whether teams meet and communicate differently knowing they may be under scrutiny by other teams. Discuss whether this affected their decision making and other aspects of "industrial spying."

● SAMPLE PLAY

1. Group is divided into three teams—Teams A, B, and C.

2. Each team receives its set of index cards (two for each round) and records the team name on the cards.

Round 1

1. Facilitator presents first problem statement.

2. Each team meets to determine and then record its response on the first card.

3. On the second card, each team records how it believes the other teams fared on their own responses.

4. Each team places their index cards face down on the table.

5. The facilitator collects both cards from each team.

6. Team A responded correctly, so Team A receives 11 points.

7. Team B responded incorrectly, so Team B receives 0 points.

8. Team C responded correctly so Team C receives 11 points.

9. Team A's predictions about Team B and Team C were that Team B would responded correctly and Team C would respond incorrectly; predictions are wrong = 0 points.

10. Team B predicted that Team A would respond correctly and Team C incorrectly. First prediction is right = 3 points; second is wrong = 0 points.

11. Team C's predictions were that Team A would be correct and Team B would be correct. One correct prediction = 3 points.

12. Total Scoring for Round 1:

Team A = 11 + 0 = 11 points;

Team B = 0 + 3 = 3 points;

Team C = 11 + 3 = 14 points.

Team C is the winner.

● CUSTOMIZING SECOND MOUSE GETS THE CHEESE

Size of Group

- For groups of six to ten, play as two teams.

- For larger groups, divide into four teams and then have each team select its "response" player(s) and its "prediction" player(s).

Time of Play

- Shorten or lengthen the time allowed for question response and predictions, depending on the size of the group.

Method of Play

- Use two different color index cards to help track the two scoring systems—one color for team responses and the second color for team predictions.

- Instruct group that each team may or may not receive a different problem. Conduct the prediction round in the same manner. Discuss how the effect of not knowing the quality of other teams' problems affected their predictions.

- Have teams prepare their prediction cards AFTER you have announced the correct response to the problem. See how this affects how each team reacts to hearing the correct response.

Scoring

- Award 7 points for predictions. Determine whether additional rewards actually undermine the quality of the responses.

Second Mouse Gets the Cheese

- **Form two to four teams.**

- **First question is presented.**

- **On the first card, write your response.**

- **On a second card, predict the quality of each of your opponent's responses.**

- **Facilitator collects both cards.**

- **Scoring:**

  Correct response = **11 points**

  Correct prediction = **3 points each**

Smack Down

....

● PURPOSE

- To create a "weakest link" situation in which you rapidly review your topic in a timed, fast-paced question-and-answer format.

● GAME OBJECTIVE

To be the team with the last icon "standing."

● PLAYERS

Six to twenty-five.

● TIME

Twenty-five to forty-five minutes.

● SUPPLIES

- One set of twenty-five or more "direct" questions for each round of play, prepared in advance by the facilitator. Direct questions prompt players to identify a fact or concept in a short response of one to five words.
- Three sets of team designator signs—A, B, C.

- Three sets of matching icons for instructor's table.

- An overhead projector (if using transparencies) or a newsprint flip chart and felt-tipped markers.

- Noise maker (optional).

- Stopwatch or timer (optional).

● GAME PLAY

1. Divide the group into two or three teams.

2. Place three icons for each team, such as a tent fold card with the team's designator (A, B, or C), on the instructor's table. For three teams this would require a total of nine icons—three A, three B, and three C icons.

3. Inform players that this game is a "lightning round," consisting of a rapid flow of questions and answers within a three-to-five-minute period.

4. Have each team select three representatives who will respond to lightning round questions.

5. Give each representative a team sign—A, B, or C. (For three teams this would require a total of nine signs.)

Rounds

1. The first question is read.

2. After 10 seconds the Team A player gives his or her response.

    A correct response keeps icons intact.

    An incorrect or no response requires one of the team's icons to be removed from the instructor's table.

3. Play is the same for Teams B and C, except that the facilitator uses a new question each time.

4. Play is the same for all rounds.

5. Declare the team with the last icon remaining the winner.

● POST-GAME DEBRIEFING

Smack Down is a good game to distinguish between knowledge that needs to be at one's fingertips (readily remembered) and those workplace situations that involve judgment calls, decision making, and problem solving. To highlight these issues, consider the following questions:

- The ability to quickly recall correct answers was the key to success today. What are some other issues in the workplace where it is important to have the right answer readily at hand?

- How do we most effectively learn the "right" answer?

- How frequently do we need to apply knowledge before it begins to slip away?

- What are some of the performance support tools or job aids you use to help you recall important facts or procedures?

- What are some of the situations on the job that call more for judgment than recall?

- How long does it typically take before a new person on the job can rely on judgment rather than procedure?

- How can we help people transition from rote memory to judgment and decision making?

● GENERAL COMMENTS

- At first glance this game appears to be complicated. But it is only a three-step process of (1) presenting the question, (2) fielding the response, and (3) removing the icon (as required). Once played this game will quickly become a favorite because of how quickly the game flows and the dynamics of the scoring, combined with the benefits of a factual recall drill.

- Use the end of each round to reinforce your instructional goal of learning and retention by going over ALL responses. This is the "moment of learning" when the participants are open to the correct responses and the rationale of the elaboration.

- Write most of the questions (80 percent) at a low level of difficulty. Use these questions in the beginning to get your players used to the flow of the game.

- Smack Down is less threatening than the highly competitive challenges featured on television. Game play encourages risk taking and promotes learning and team spirit.

- To further enhance learning and retention make the questions visible to players by placing them on charts, overheads, or PowerPoint® presentations.

- Have participants contribute questions for game play. Using participant questions gives you an idea of their perspective on the topic as well as helping you reduce your question preparation time.

● SAMPLE PLAY

1. Group is divided into two teams—A and B.

2. Each team selects three player-representatives, each of whom receive a team designator card—A or B.

3. Facilitator sets up three team icons for each team on a table.

Round 1: First Players for Each Team

1. The first question is presented.

2. The Team A player responds correctly within 10 seconds.

3. The team icon remains standing.

4. The second question is presented.

5. The Team B player responds incorrectly within 10 seconds.

6. One Team B icon is removed.

Round 2: Second Players for Each Team

1. The third question is presented.

2. The Team A player gives no response within 10 seconds. This is scored the same as an incorrect response, and a Team A icon is removed.

A		B	A	B

3. The fourth question is presented.

4. The Team B player responds correctly within 10 seconds.

5. The team icon remains standing.

A		B	A	B

Rest of Game

1. Play continues as above.

2. The last team with a standing icon wins the game.

● CUSTOMIZING SMACK DOWN

Size of Group

- For small groups of six to ten, form two teams of three to five players each and then have the teams select three players to represent them during the question-and-answer session.

- For larger groups, form three teams and then have teams select the players to represent them.

Time of Play

- Expand the time of the round to allow for longer response times (15 seconds or more) or additional questions.

Method of Play

- Use the beam of light created by a flashlight or laser light to select players for each round. The facilitator normally would hold the light source, but this could be delegated to team leaders or players from opposing teams.

Scoring

- Establish point value questions of 10, 20, and 30 points. Scoring can be a combination of points AND bonus points for standing icons.

Smack Down

....

- Group divides into two or three teams.

- Each team selects three player representatives.

- Facilitator sets up three icons for each team.

- Facilitator reads a question.

- First player has 10 seconds to reply.

- Scoring: If the response is . . .

    Correct, end of turn.

    Incorrect, remove one team icon.

- Second and third players each get a turn.

- The team with the last icon standing wins.

Speed Dial

● ●

● **PURPOSE**

- To create a dialog about personal values.

- To create a dialog about key contacts in our lives.

● **GAME OBJECTIVE**

To create a list of the most important values.

● **PLAYERS**

Eight or more.

● **TIME**

Twenty-five to forty-five minutes.

● **SUPPLIES**

- A Planning Sheet for each participant.

- Two extra Planning Sheets for each team.

- A pen or pencil for each participant.

- An overhead projector (if using transparencies) or a newsprint flip chart and felt-tipped markers.

- Noisemaker (optional).

- Stopwatch or timer (optional).

● GAME PLAY

1. Divide the group into two or more teams of four to six players per team.

2. Distribute one Planning Sheet and a pen or pencil to each participant.

3. First, ask each participant to fill out the Planning Sheet, listing five people who would be on the speed dial of their cell phones and why.

   - Who? Designation (spouse, children, doctor, etc.)

   - Why? Why should this person be included?

   - What values does this person represent for you?

4. After 5 minutes, ask participants if they mind sharing their speed dial lists with the rest of the team. Start flip charts to identify and group similarities for the people or reasons. Groupings may reflect the same people (spouses, children, friends, and parents) or they may reflect similar values (importance of family, work responsibilities, self-care).

5. Next, distribute two additional Planning Sheets to each team.

6. Ask each team to create one representative speed dial list that reflects the shared values of the team. For instance, is it an agreed-on value that the boss should be notified if you are going to be late or must miss work? Does it seem that everyone on the team places a high value on their family being aware of their whereabouts?

7. After 5 minutes ask each team to present its list.

8. Ask each team to regroup and create a speed dial list for its office, division, or company.

9. After 7 minutes, ask each team to present its list.

● POST-GAME DEBRIEFING

Speed Dial can be debriefed in several ways. Here are three different models:

1. Focus on our workplace network of contacts. Most of us have a network of people at work. Ask:

   - Who do you call when you want to get the straight story about what is going on? Why did you pick that person?

   - Who do you call when you want to figure out the politics of a situation? Why did you pick that person?

   - Who do you call when you need a sounding board so that you can gripe or blow off steam or test out a new idea? Why is this useful?

   - Who do you call when you need advice or guidance? Do you consider these people coaches or mentors?

   - How might you go about finding such people and where might they be found in your organization?

2. Use as a venue to identify critical stakeholders or responsible people in your company. Used in this way, Speed Dial can reinforce who is responsible for what when orienting new hires to an organization. The following questions are examples of this application:

   - Who would you call if a customer called threatening to sue?

   - Who would you call if an employee were threatening others with a gun?

   - Who would you call if you smelled smoke in a stairway?

3. Use as a means to explore other organizational priorities. For example, you might ask:

   - Who would/should be on the team leader's speed dial?

   - Who would/should be on the CEO/president's/other executive's speed dial?

● GENERAL COMMENTS

- The point of Speed Dial is to raise a topic rarely discussed in teams—the importance and impact of our individual and collective values.

- It was a poignant insight into the role of technology in our lives when we heard of 9/11 last-minute cell phone calls to loved ones. The premise of Speed Dial is that, when the chips are down, the question "Who you gonna call?" (to quote *Ghost Busters*) is significant. The answer to that question reveals a great deal about our values, our relationships, and what matters most to us. Speed Dial brings into sharp focus those values we share in common and is an intriguing lead in to any discussion of work/life balance.

- Without becoming overly intrusive, Speed Dial serves to surface those deeply held internal values and enable us to find commonality with our colleagues. Shared values, not just organizational affiliation or similar work titles, bind us together. Speed Dial offers teams an important productivity boost by helping them explore just what values they do hold in common. It also helps teammates better appreciate the values and motivations of their colleagues.

- In facilitating Speed Dial there is really no element of competition. Participants are getting to know one another via a discussion of their values, their relationships, and the people who matter most in their lives.

● CUSTOMIZING SPEED DIAL

Size of Group

- For groups of six to ten, play as two teams.

- For larger groups, play as prescribed.

Time of Play

- Shorten or lengthen the time allowed for team meetings and presentations, as necessary.

Method of Play

- Have groups form by offices and have each office develop a speed dial. Have the offices compare their lists with each other and discuss what other offices are on their speed dials.

- Have teams create lists for a specific situation, such as developing a new budget, managing a new project, a new product launch, executive recruiting, and so forth.

- Have teams create lists from five or ten years ago.

- Have teams create lists for ten years in the future.

- Have group create one list of seven common contacts from all the lists.

- **Divide into two or more teams.**

- **List five people who should be on your personal cell phone's speed dial.**

- **Meet with your team and then make a representative list of five people who should be on your speed dial list.**

- **Meet again with your team and create a speed dial list for your company.**

- **Present your team's speed dial list to the rest of the group.**

Speed Dial

. . . .

If you were given a new cell phone with a speed dial for five people, who would you place on the speed dial?

1. Name or Designation: _____
   Why is this person on my speed dial?

2. Name or Designation: _____
   Why is this person on my speed dial?

3. Name or Designation: _____
   Why is this person on my speed dial?

4. Name or Designation: _____
   Why is this person on my speed dial?

5. Name or Designation: _____
   Why is this person on my speed dial?

Splitting Hares

· ·

● **PURPOSE**

- To stimulate effective team problem solving by focusing on the ultimate outcome as well as the means of problem solving.

- To prompt teams to ask more questions and to develop better questioning skills.

● **GAME OBJECTIVE**

To resolve the problem as correctly as possible.

● **PLAYERS**

Six or more.

● **TIME**

Fifteen to thirty minutes.

● **SUPPLIES**

- One "problem" item (raw egg or lemon or lime or orange) per team. Each team should receive the same item.

- One Problem Worksheet for each team.

- One Facilitator Guide, to help you respond to team queries.

- An overhead projector (if using transparencies) or a newsprint flip chart and felt-tipped markers.

- Pencils or pens for each team.

- Stopwatch and whistle (optional).

● GAME PLAY

1. Divide into two or more teams.

2. Distribute the "problem item," a Problem Worksheet, and a pen or pencil to each team.

3. Explain the task.

   - Each team has 5 minutes to produce the best possible solution to the problem stated on the sheet.

   - During the 5-minute period, each team is allowed to verbally ask two questions of the facilitator, whose reply can only be "yes" or "no."

   - Facilitator will share all questions and responses with the entire group.

   - At the end of 5 minutes teams are to turn in their proposed solutions.

4. Tell teams to begin.

5. Call time at the end of 5 minutes.

6. Ask all teams to submit their proposed solution.

7. Review the solutions with the group and determine which team produced the fairest solution.

● POST-GAME DEBRIEFING

Critical questions teams should ask in attempting to solve problems include:

- *Ownership:* Who "owns" this problem? In coming up with your answers, who seemed to "own" the problem?

- *Stake:* How invested are stakeholders in reaching a solution? Did someone on your team seem to have a strong stake in his or her answer being accepted as the team answer?

- *Win/Win:* Must solutions for two parties be mutually incompatible?

- *Urgency:* How fast must we reach a solution? What was the impact of time pressure on your decision-making processes in this game?

- *Criticality:* How critical is it that we get the solution right the first time? What was your strategy for determining what was the "right" answer?

- *Limitations:* What are we specifically precluded from doing? Did anyone on your team make a point of listing limitations?

- *Definition of Success:* What constitutes a "successful solution" from the perspective of the parties involved?

- *Rules:* What are the rules? How did your team attempt to bend them, reinterpret them, dodge them, or break them without getting caught?

- *Negotiation:* Can engaging one or more parties to the problem alter the nature of the problem or the potential solution set?

- *Properties:* Sometimes it's essential to know about facts of the problem, numbers, size, weight, dimensions, volume, temperature, material, and so forth. For example, what if the egg to be divided is a plastic egg filled with miniature chocolates or marshmallow "peeps"?

● GENERAL COMMENTS

- As Solomon demonstrated when asked to divide one baby between two women, the solution for any problem may depend on the interests and equities of the individuals involved. Simple mathematics, logic, or sheer creativity may be inadequate to resolve a problem unless you take the time to learn the reasons behind the problem and to define what constitutes a successful outcome (and from whose perspective). Splitting Hares is a lively way to engage people in looking at the problem "behind the problem" and in honing their questioning skills to uncover that critical information.

- Note that we all have favorite questions that we invariably start with. One of the co-authors of this book invariably starts by trying to evade the rules by understanding limitations. Knowing how we habitually approach problem solving from the kinds of questions we generally ask offers ways to improve team performance. Creating a profile of how different team members approach problem solving improves the team's overall chances of success by bringing the team's natural diversity of talent to bear.

● SAMPLE PLAY

1. The group is divided into three teams—Team A, Team B, and Team C.

2. Each team receives an item—an egg—along with a Problem Worksheet and a pen or pencil.

3. The facilitator informs the teams that they must provide a remedy that would divide the egg equitably between two households. Furthermore, the raw egg cannot be substantially altered to accomplish the task. The teams are informed that they may ask two "yes" or "no" questions.

4. Team A asks its first question:

   "Do both households want to use the egg in preparation of food?"

5. The facilitator responds: "Yes."

6. All teams enter the response on their worksheets.

7. Team C asks its first question:

   "Can we boil the egg?"

8. The facilitator responds: "No."

9. Team B asks its first question:

   "Can we scramble the egg?"

10. The facilitator responds: "No."

11. Team C asks its second question:

    "Can we freeze the egg before dividing it?"

12. The facilitator responds: "No."

13. Team A asks its second question:

    "Can we puree it in a blender, add Tabasco sauce and tomato juice, and take it as a hangover cure?"

14. The facilitator responds: "No."

15. Team B asks its second question:

   "Do both households want to use the same part of the egg?"

16. The facilitator responds: "No."

17. The facilitator calls time after 5 minutes.

18. The three teams submit their proposed solutions:

   - Team A proposes to carefully divide the shell and weigh each portion of the raw egg and then distribute it to the two households.

   - Team B proposes to divide the raw egg—inside and shell—and then distribute it to the households.

   - Team C proposes to crack the egg and give the inside to one household and the shell to the other household.

19. The facilitator announces that Team C's solution is the fairest and most equitable.

● CUSTOMIZING SPLITTING HARES

Size of Group

- For groups of six to ten, divide into two teams. Allow two or more questions per team.

- For larger groups of twenty-five to fifty, divide into as many as eight teams, but allow only one question per team.

Time of Play

- Shorten or lengthen the time allowed for questions or problem solution.

Method of Play

- Give a brief lecture on questioning techniques prior to playing the game.

- Use only one "problem" item by holding it up to the class and allowing them to handle the item at their tables, as necessary.

- Allow only one question for each team. This will increase the importance of selecting and phrasing their only opportunity to acquire information about the scenario from the facilitator.

- Allow each team three questions. They must submit the questions in writing, and the response will be provided in writing, but ONLY to the inquiring team. This will reinforce the concept of knowledge management. Observe how teams choose to share their responses, if at all, with the other teams.

- Allow additional time for question and response. When the teams are finished making their inquiries, then start the 5-minute problem solution period.

Scoring

- Charge each team 10 points for each question asked. Deduct these points from the points awarded for the best solution.

- Award points for the best (25), second-best (15) and third-best (5) solutions.

PLAYER INSTRUCTIONS FOR
Splitting Hares

. . . .

- **Form two or more teams.**

- **Distribute item and Problem Worksheet.**

- **Each team has 5 minutes to construct solution fairest to all parties involved.**

- **Each team is allowed two yes-or-no questions.**

- **Time called at the end of 5 minutes.**

- **Each team presents its solution to the group.**

- **Solution(s) that is fairest to both parties is the winner.**

PROBLEM WORKSHEET FOR
Splitting Hares

• •

- You are a judge in small claims court.

- Two households claim ownership of the object you have been provided.

- You have 5 minutes to develop the fairest solution for BOTH households.

- During the problem-solving period, each team is allowed to ask the facilitator two questions whose answers can only be "Yes" or "No."

- The facilitator will share all questions and responses with the rest of the group.

- At the end of 5 minutes you are to turn in your problem solution.

Question Posed to Facilitator: _____

Response: _____

Conclusion: _____

Question: _____

Response: _____

Conclusion: _____

Question: _____

Response: _____

Conclusion: _____

Question: _____

Response: _____

Conclusion: _____

Question: _____

Response: _____

Conclusion: _____

FACILITATOR GUIDE FOR
Splitting Hares

The following explains how each household will use the item in question.

Lime

- Household A wants one-quarter section of a lime to run around the top of their margarita glasses before dredging them in salt.

- Household B wants the juice from three-quarters of a lime to make key lime pie for dessert and the rind of three-quarters of a lime to use as zest in the meringue topping.

Lemon

- Household A wants the pulp of the lemon for lemonade.

- Household B wants the lemon rind for a cake.

Orange

- Household A wants the pulp of the orange for juice.

- Household B wants the orange rind for a cake.

Egg

- Household A wants the egg yolk and egg white for a cake mix.

- Household B wants the eggshell to brew with the coffee grounds.

Tattoo

. . . .

● **PURPOSE**

- To create a dialog about the different images we hold of an organization as new hires and how those images change as we become seasoned employees.

● **GAME OBJECTIVE**

To create the best company tattoo.

● **PLAYERS**

Eight or more.

● **TIME**

Twenty to thirty-five minutes.

● **SUPPLIES**

- One set of Planning Sheets per team, one for each team member plus one for the team.
- Pen or pencil for each participant.

- An overhead projector (if using transparencies) or a newsprint flip chart and felt-tipped markers.

- Stopwatch and whistle.

● GAME PLAY

1. Divide the group into two or more teams of four to six players per team.

2. Distribute one set of Planning Sheets to each team.

3. Ask each participant to plan a tattoo that reflects his or her company and to fill out the planning sheet specifying:

    - *Words:* What words (maximum of four) would they have inscribed?

    - *Design:* What design would they select?

    - *Placement:* Where would they have the tattoo placed?

4. After 5 minutes, ask participants if they mind sharing their tattoos with the rest of their team.

5. Ask each team to use the extra Planning Sheet to create a single representative tattoo.

6. After 10 minutes ask each team to present and explain the significance of its tattoo to the rest of the group.

7. Post all tattoos on the wall and have the group select the best tattoo—the tattoo they would wear as a tee-shirt.

● POST-GAME DEBRIEFING

Ask the group:

- How did you feel during the exercise?

- What design did you pick and why?

- What word or words did you select and why?

- Where did you place the tattoo and why?

- What was your image of the organization before you were hired?

- How did that image change as you learned more about the organization and its culture?

- What has surprised you most since you joined the organization?

- How is your image of the organization different now than it was five or ten years ago?

- What is the strongest element of the image you have at this point?

- What mysteries are you still hoping to have explained to you?

Another application of Tattoo is to explore public or customer views of the organization. Ask:

- What is the image that the public (customers) hold of the organization?

- What is the impact of this publicly held image?

- What might we do to change this image?

● GENERAL COMMENTS

- There is nothing more personal, or more permanent, than a tattoo. One's own attitude is as permanent, but not as visible, as a tattoo. This exercise asks participants to visualize something that would be a part of their persona, more than any piece of jewelry or article of clothing. This is a personal perspective of the mission and goals of the company—something they would "wear" or carry on their bodies forever.

- Tattoos carry a variety of connotations—both positive and negative. Tattoos are often seen as playful or reckless—an expression of youth, a military experience, or ritual of a social club or gang. It may remind some people of oppression and prison camps—especially those of World War II. Here we ask participants to adopt a tattoo that reflects their view of where they work and what they believe. Remind those players that this is a visualization exercise and that the tattoo is only being used because of its "permanence." In addition, no one is required, or will even be asked, to adopt the tattoo.

- This exercise can elicit a visual composite of the organization—how different divisions and functions "see" the organization. For mid-career or seasoned employees, Tattoo can be a novel way to explore the changing attitudes we develop toward our organization the longer we are part of it. In facilitating this discussion, draw out the situations, the experiences, the challenges employees have encountered that led them to change their initial view of the organization.

- Bring in washable tattoos as samples.

● CUSTOMIZING TATTOO

Size of Group

- For groups from six to ten, play as two teams.

- For larger groups, play as prescribed.

Time of Play

- Shorten or lengthen the time allowed for team meetings and presentations, as necessary.

Method of Play

- Have teams create "special event" tattoos for the promotion of the new product, move to a new location, merger with another company, or other events.

- Have teams create their tattoos on quarter sheets of paper and attach the design to their clothing during the exercise.

Scoring

- Have group select the best tattoo by categories:

    Most Unique

    Most Humorous

    Best Conversation Starter

    Most Likely to Be Worn by the Executives

    Least Likely to Be Worn by the Executives

Tattoo

- **Form two or more teams.**

- **Plan a personal tattoo.**

- **If you wish, share your tattoo and design with the rest of your team.**

- **Now create one tattoo that represents your team.**

- **Present your team's tattoo to the rest of the group.**

PLANNING SHEET FOR
Tattoo

• •

The company is asking you to consider wearing your own company tattoo. Please use this Planning Sheet to decide on your tattoo.

- What words (up to four) do you want inscribed?

  _____   _____   _____   _____

- What design or picture do you want in the tattoo?
  (draw or describe)

- Where (on your body) will the tattoo be placed?

Team Poker

• •

● PURPOSE

- To explore the dynamics of sharing versus competition.

- To encourage discussion about individual and team objectives.

● GAME OBJECTIVE

To have the most team points at the end of the game.

● PLAYERS

Four or more, in groups of four.

● TIME

Thirty-five to fifty-five minutes.

● SUPPLIES

- One ordinary deck of playing cards, per set of teams.

- One Ranking Chart of winning poker hands per set of teams.

- One Score Sheet per set of teams.

- An overhead projector (if using transparencies) or a newsprint flip chart and felt-tipped markers for posting the scores.

- Paper and pencils for each team.

- One timer and call bell.

● GAME PLAY

1. Divide the participants into groups of four, each comprised of two two-person teams. If possible, have the two teams face each other across a small table.

2. Distribute one deck of cards, one Ranking Chart, one Score Sheet, and a pen or pencil to each table.

3. Have teams select a dealer; the dealer distributes cards during game play. (Dealer rotates clockwise for subsequent rounds.)

Round 1: Distribution of Cards

1. The dealer distributes four cards to each player, including him- or herself, placing each card face down (design side up) on the table.

2. The dealer then places three common cards—cards that can be used by any of the players—face up in the middle of the table.

3. The object for each player is to form the best poker hand from any combination of four cards in their hand PLUS the three common cards on the table.

Round 1: Card Exchange—Forming the Best Poker Hand

1. The first player to the left of the dealer has the option of trading any one of his or her cards for one of the three common cards.

2. If the player does NOT wish to trade, he or she simply says: "Pass."

3. If the player wants to trade, he or she says: "Trade" and then . . .

- Takes one of his or her (face down) cards and places this card face up in the center. This represents a new common card that can be used by all other players.

- Takes one of the common cards from the table and places it face-up with his or her own hand. Although all players can see the card, the player who made the trade is the only one who can use this card.

4. The process of "trade" or "pass" goes once around the table and then continues until two consecutive players say: "Pass."

5. Each player then forms the best five-card poker hand.

Scoring

1. As determined by the Ranking Chart, the player with the:

- Best hand receives 10 points.

- Second-best hand receives 5 points.

- Third-best hand receives 3 points.

- Fourth-best hand receives 1 point.

2. Teams tally and post their points on the Score Card.

Subsequent Rounds

1. Play is the same for all rounds.

2. The team of players with the most points wins.

● POST-GAME DEBRIEFING

This game encourages the strategy that it is not always best to collect all the resources for your own hand—that a winning strategy could be to keep the resources as "common cards" for other players, especially your partner. In this game you are never sure whether your partner is building his or her hand or trying to help you build yours. And of course, you and your partner are always trying to confound the opposing team's effort to build their best hands.

Some interesting processing points arise from this effort. Among them are the following:

- Which was more important, that you won or that you and your partner won? Why do you say so?

- What role did shared resources (the face cards in the middle of the table) play in your attempt to build a winning hand? In our day-to-day work, how can we use shared resources more effectively?

- In attempting to strengthen your partner's hand, how did you know what to offer him or her? How do you know what is of use (or no use) to your partner or your opponent? What sort of strategies do we fall back on when it becomes clear that our partners do not share our strategies?

- In our day-to-day work, how can we learn how to play to someone else's strengths and how can we communicate our own strengths?

- When we put someone else in a "one up" or "one down" position—either intentionally or by accident—what are the likely consequences?

- How can we make our intentions clear? In this group, how do we typically communicate what we want/need or do not want/do not need?

- When we want the other side (another unit, division, or function) to understand where we are coming from, what are some of the ways we can check for understanding?

- What arguments or rationales are most likely to persuade the people with whom we most frequently interact?

- In this game, the rules of poker determine the value of each card and define what constitutes a winning hand. Within our organizational or team culture, what determines the value of the "cards" we hold? What is it that our culture values most?

- What constitutes an "unbeatable hand" in our culture?

- How do we define "winning"? Do we generally focus on "winning" as an individual, as a team, as a functional group of some kind, or as an entire organization?

- Imagine that you played this game with all cards face-up on the table. How might you have played differently if your motives—to assemble a power hand or disrupt your opponent's hand—were transparent to the entire group?

● GENERAL COMMENTS

- This game is best when played for three or more rounds. This gives players the opportunity to see the relationship between strategy and score.

- Reasons to trade with common cards (the center cards that can be used in anyone's hand):

    The common card will strengthen your own hand.

    To remove a common card you think will help your opponent.

    To insert a card in the common cards that might help your partner.

    To void your own hand of poor or unusable cards.

- Additional rounds of play usually provide players with valuable insights on self-help through collaborative behavior. This mindset can be paralleled with the concept of "team play," where each player tries not just to improve his or her own hand, but looks at how to improve the best hand on his or her team.

- Some players may not be familiar with the rules of poker. A sample round of play can familiarize players with both the rules of the game and the Ranking Chart.

- The second and subsequent series of trades can continue only if two or more players are willing to continue to play. What happens if members of your organization decide to just "stand pat" and passively watch as you try to improve your teams' hands?

- Some players may refuse to play, citing the aversion to anything associated with gambling. Encourage these players to act as monitors and observers of play. Their role is to record and report (if needed) how the players reacted to the reverse winning role required by the game.

- One of the benefits of Team Poker is that it can be used to facilitate a discussion of what "winning" really means and what kind of information needs to be routinely exchanged if we attempt a "group win."

- Organizations and teams do not always play to win. Sometimes individuals play more to maximize their individual performance than to optimize benefits for the group as a whole. Some examples of this behavior include managers who:

    "Pad" employees' performance appraisals so that they look like better performers than they are.

    Routinely assign their least experienced or capable people to any task force, matrix-group, or joint effort.

    Underestimate the amount of time/resources required by a project so that some other team will pick it up.

● SAMPLE PLAY

1. Group of four is divided into two teams of two players each—Team A and Team B.

2. The dealer, A1, distributes four cards, face down, to each player and then places three cards face up in the center.

First Hand

- Player B1 = J spades, J clubs, 7 hearts, 2 clubs

- Player A2 = K spades, 9 diamonds, 5 clubs, 3 hearts

- Player B2 = K diamonds, Q hearts, J hearts, 6 clubs

- Player A1 (dealer) = K hearts, 6 spades, 4 hearts, 2 hearts

- Common cards = 10 hearts, 7 clubs, 3 clubs

First Series: Trade or Pass

Player B1: Trade

- The first player to the left of the dealer says: "Trade" and then exchanges her 2 clubs for the 7 clubs. She places the 7 clubs face up.

- Player B1 now holds: J spades, J clubs, 7 hearts, and 7 clubs.

Player A2: Trade

- The player facing the dealer says: "Trade" and then exchanges his 9 diamonds for the 3 clubs. He places the 3 clubs face up.

- Player A2 now holds: K spades, 5 clubs, 3 hearts, and 3 clubs.

Player B2: Trade

- The player to the right of the dealer says: "Trade" and then exchanges his 6 clubs for the 10 hearts. He places the 10 hearts face up.

- Player B2 now holds: K diamonds, Q hearts, J hearts, and 10 hearts.

Player A1: Trade

- The dealer says: "Trade" and then exchanges his 4 hearts for the 6 clubs. He places the 6 clubs face up.

- Player A2 now holds: K hearts, 6 spades, 6 clubs, and 2 hearts.

- After the first series of trades, the common cards are: 9 diamonds, 4 hearts, and 2 clubs.

Second Series: Trade or Pass

Player B1: Pass

- Player B1 is holding two pairs—J spades and J clubs, 7 hearts and 7 clubs. There are no common cards that can improve his hand.

Player A2: Trade

- Player A2 hopes to improve his chances for a straight, so he trades the K spades for the 4 hearts. He places the 4 hearts face up.

- Player A2 now holds: 5 clubs, 4 hearts, 3 hearts, and 3 clubs.

Player B2: Pass

- Player B2 is holding a possible straight—K diamonds, Q hearts, J hearts, and 10 hearts in his hand. Matched with the common card, 9 diamonds, this would make a straight.

Player A1: Trade

- The dealer says: "Trade" and then exchanges his 2 hearts for the K spades. He places the K spades face up.

- Player A1 now holds 2 pair: K spades, K hearts, 6 spades, and 6 clubs.

- After the second series of trades, the common cards are: 9 diamonds, 2 hearts, and 2 clubs.

Third Series: Trade or Pass

Player B1: Pass

- Player B1 is still holding two pairs—J spades and J clubs, 7 hearts and 7 clubs. There are no common cards that can improve his hand.

Player A2: Trade

- Player A2 continues to hope to improve his chances for a straight, so he trades the 3 hearts for the 2 hearts. He places the 2 hearts face up.

- Player A2 now holds: 5 clubs, 4 hearts, 3 clubs, and 2 hearts.
  (*Note:* Player A2 knows that his partner, A1, holds at least one six (the 6 clubs, showing face up) and hopes that his partner can place a 6 in the common cards.)

Player B2: Pass

- Player B2 is holding onto a straight (10 to K, in his hand) and 9 as a common card.

Play A1: Pass

- Dealer holds two pairs—Kings and sixes—in his hand. He does not pick up on "cue" from his team member, A2.

End of Round

- Since two players have now passed, the round ends.

Scoring

** = common card

- B2: best hand = straight (K diamonds, Q hearts, J hearts, 10 hearts, 9 diamonds**) = 10 points

- A1: second-best hand = 2 pairs: Kings and sixes (K spades, K hearts, 6 spaces, 6 clubs) = 5 points

- B1: third-best hand = 2 pairs: Jacks and sevens (J spades, J clubs, 7 hearts, 7 clubs) = 3 points

- A2: fourth-best hand = 2 pairs: threes and deuces (3 hearts**, 3 clubs, 2 hearts, 2 clubs**) = 1 point

Score After Round 1

- Team B = 10 + 3 = 13 points

- Team A = 5 + 1 = 6 points

● CUSTOMIZING TEAM POKER

Size of Group

- For smaller groups, play one or two sets of games simultaneously.

- For larger groups conduct simultaneous games. To avoid undue confusion, conduct one sample "fishbowl" round of play using four players while the rest of the participants observe; then entertain questions about the rules, roles, or ranking of the hands, as required.

- If necessary, have each team conduct its own sample round of play, with all cards facing up.

Time of Play

- Expand the number of rounds of play to five or more.

- Allow additional time depending on the group size and/or their familiarity with card games.

Method of Play

- Assign a secret role to one or more players per team. For example, you might tell one player:

  "The player on your right is your boss. You must try to lose as many hands as possible to protect your boss from the 'loss of face' of not winning in front of his or her subordinates."

- If your players have an aversion to using ordinary playing cards (form of gambling, etc.), simply write out four sets of the numbers 1 to 10 on ordinary index cards, using four colors (red, green, black, blue) as the suits.

Scoring

- Change the scoring to allow for ties after a round of play.

  - Best = 7 points

  - Second-best = 5 points

  - Third-best = 3 points

  - Fourth-best = 1 point

    (The Best + Fourth-Best = Second-Best + Third-Best.)

- Determine whether the possibility of a tie creates even more competitive play. If so, why?

Team Poker

....

- Form sets of two two-person teams.

- Each player receives four cards (face down), and then three "common" cards are placed face up in the middle of the table.

- Each player, in turn, may trade any one of his or her cards for one common card.

- Round ends when two consecutive players "pass."

- Form your best five-card poker hand from your four cards AND the three common cards.

Best hand =	10 points
Second-best hand =	5 points
Third-best hand =	3 points
Fourth-best hand =	1 point

- Tally the team score.

- The team with the most points wins.

RANKING CHART FOR
Team Poker

Cards/Suits Ranked in Order of Value (Highest to Lowest)

(A) Ace

(K) King

(Q) Queen

(J) Jack

(10) Ten

(9) Nine

(8) Eight

(7) Seven

(6) Six

(5) Five

(4) Four

(3) Three

(2) Two

Spades (s)

Hearts (h)

Diamonds (d)

Clubs (c)

Winning Hands Ranked in Order of Power (Highest to Lowest)

Royal Flush—Straight flush made up of A, K, Q, J, and 10 in same suit.

Straight Flush—Five cards of the same suit in numerical order—6d, 7d, 8d, 9d, 10d.

Four of a Kind—Four cards of the same rank—four Jacks (Js, Jh, Jd, Jc).

Full House—Three of a kind AND a pair—for example, three 8's (8, 8, 8) and two 4's (4, 4). In case of two full houses, the highest three of a kind wins.

Flush—Five cards of the same suit not in sequence—Kc, Jc, 8c, 5c, 4c.

Straight—Five cards in sequence with mixed suits—6c, 7d, 8c, 9s, 10h.

Three of a Kind—Three cards of a kind—for example, Q, Q, Q. In case of two or more three of a kinds, the highest value cards win.

Two Pair—Two sets of pairs—for example, two 8's, (8, 8) and two 5's (5, 5). In case of two matching hands, the highest set of pairs wins (10h, 10d beats 8h, 8d or 7h, 7s).

One Pair—One set of two of a kind—for example, two Jacks (J, J). In case of matching hands, the highest pair wins.

SCORE SHEET FOR
Team Poker

	Player A1	Player A2	Team A Total	Team B Total	Player B1	Player B2
Round 1						
Round 2						
Round 3						
Round 4						
Round 5						
Round 6						

Virtual X-Change

· ·

● PURPOSE

- To demonstrate the challenges of distance collaboration.

- To demonstrate the importance of inter-team communication.

● GAME OBJECTIVE

To obtain a collaborative Tic-Tac-Toe on the Master Game Sheet.

● PLAYERS

Six or more, divided into three teams.

● TIME

Twenty-five to fifty-five minutes.

● SUPPLIES

- One Master Game Sheet, for the facilitator to track the spaces selected by the three teams for each round.

- Two sets of three Game Sheets, preferably in three separate colors—one Game Sheet for each playing team; the second copy of each Game Sheet is kept by the facilitator.

- One set of Message Sheets for each team, preferably to match the Game Sheet issued to each team.

- An overhead projector (if using transparencies) or a newsprint flip chart and felt-tipped markers.

- Tent fold cards for team identification.

- Flip chart easel and felt-tipped markers.

- Timer and noisemaker (optional).

- Stapler.

● PREPARATION

Prepare one set of Game Sheets (two copies of three Game Sheets):

- Select any three of the four Game Sheets so that each team receives a different Game Sheet. The Game Sheet title is followed by one to four dots. These dots, all but invisible to the players, are reminders for you of the different space numbering system used.

- Create two copies of each Game Sheet, preferably in three different colors of your choice. Give one copy of a Game Sheet to each playing team; keep the second copy. Since teams will communicate their space selections only by number, the extra copy helps you translate each team's number into a selected space on the Master Game Sheet.

Create one set of Message Sheets:

- Photocopy the page with eight copies in three colors, each color matching a Game Sheet. The matching colors—Game Sheet and Message Sheet—will help you to identify and translate each team's numerical selections as well as providing a team "identity."

- Create the set of messages by cutting each of the Message Sheets into eight separate message slips and then stapling each set of eight slips, if possible.

● GAME PLAY

1. Divide the group into three teams, seating each team in a different section of the room.

2. Distribute a tent fold card and matching Game Sheet and set of Message Sheets to each team.

3. Have each team create a team name and place it on its tent fold.

4. Place the Master Game Sheet out of sight.

5. Post a blank three-by-three Tic-Tac-Toe grid on an overhead transparency, flip chart, or chalkboard to indicate when the three teams have collaboratively selected a space.

6. Inform the three teams that their task is to create a collaborative Tic-Tac-Toe on the Master Game Sheet, one space at a time.

7. For each round have each team select one space on its own Game Sheet without discussion with any other team and then hand you a Virtual Message with the space number.

8. As you receive a Virtual Message, first compare the team selection to the appropriate team Game Sheet and then record the selection on the Master Game Sheet.

9. If the three selections . . .

   - *Occur on the Same Space.* Mark an "X" on the flip chart Game Sheet space visible to all teams. This completes the round.

   - *Differ.* Take no action. This completes the round.

   - *Occur in Two Spaces.* Inform teams that two marks match, but one mark differs. Teams have *one chance* to select the same space, but only by exchanging Virtual Messages.

10. Have teams meet again (separately) and send one message to each of the other two teams.

    The messages must be written on a Virtual Message form and may contain only words or numbers—no drawings—in *three words/numbers or fewer.*

11. Tell teams to crumple their completed Virtual Message forms and then toss them to the other two teams.

---

12. Each team records its second selection and hands it to you. Compare the numbers:

   • If all teams select the same space, mark a space on the flip chart Game Sheet. This ends the round.

   • If the teams DO NOT select the same space, mark no spaces on the flip chart. This ends the round.

Subsequent Rounds

   1. All rounds are played in a similar fashion.

   2. If the teams cannot select the same space within two selections, this ends the round.

   3. Call time when the teams successfully create a Tic-Tac-Toe on the flip chart game sheet or after seven rounds of play.

● POST-GAME DEBRIEFING

The following questions will focus participants on communication issues:

   • What type of information were you specifically looking for?

   • Did you send this same type of information to other teams? Why or why not?

   • Did you send data about the Game Sheet? Why or why not?

   • How did you go about clarifying the information you wanted to receive from other teams?

   • Did you assume that you were all using the same terms in the same way? If not, how did you go about checking your assumptions?

   • Did you assume that the other teams were looking at a similar game board to yours? How did you check or test out that assumption?

   • Did you assume that other teams wanted the same information that you wanted? Why was that?

   • Did you experience any of the following failures in communication?

      Failure to explain terms.

      Failure to explain the situation.

Failure to explain what was meant.

Failure to deliver the message.

Failure to deliver the message to the right person.

● GENERAL COMMENTS

- Requiring teams to submit their selected spaces by "numbers" infers that there is only one numbering system. The discovery of multiple numbering systems typically prompts teams to reconsider whether or not all teams are working with the same data, the same rules, or the same picture of reality.

- There are four different Game Sheets. Each of the sheets is numbered differently to simulate the many misinterpretations inherent in virtual exchanges—language barriers, differences in interpretations and semantics, asynchronous time, geographic distance, and so on. When teams discover not everyone is on the same "page," they begin to learn how to articulate and test their assumptions and to accommodate for differences—the first step to virtual teaming.

- Using different color Game Sheets may inspire teams to select names that reflect their team color, such as "Blue Crew," "Mellow Yellow," "Purple Gang," "Pink Floyds," and others.

- There may be frustration in the beginning when "obvious" messages are being ignored or not understood by the other teams. Consider assisting the teams to realize that virtual teams must deal with many challenges, the least of which is distance.

- Having the teams write their messages on a Message Sheet and then crumple the sheet and throw it to the other teams simulates electronic transfer of messages.

- Teams initially may think they are competing against each other. You may wish to cover this in different ways—restating the objective of the exercise, allowing the teams to play one or two rounds and discover that they want to select the exact space to create three in a row in order to win.

- Teams sometimes create "SPAM"—messages that do not have anything to do with the exercise. This can parallel real-life receipt of useless data.

● CUSTOMIZING VIRTUAL X-CHANGE

Size of Group

- For groups of six to nine, play as two- or three-person teams.

- For larger groups of twenty-five to fifty, split the group into two rounds, assigning the teams sitting out the round to observe one of the playing teams. Then reverse the roles on the second round. The debriefing can cover what behaviors the observing teams noted during the rounds of play.

Time of Play

- Shorten or lengthen the time allowed for presentation of the tasks, depending on the difficulty of the computation.

Method of Play

- Create separate instruction sheets for each team, including:

    Tips ("Always select the center space first").

    Tasks to be performed ("Tell the other teams to select upper row only").

    Encouragement ("Go outside the rules. Use as many words as you need; the three-word rule is wrong").

Scoring

- Award 1 point to the two teams who select the same space; determine whether this is considered "favoritism" by the players.

Virtual X-Change

....

- **Form three teams.**

- ***Objective:* Create a Tic-Tac-Toe on the Master Game Sheet.**

- **Each team selects a space on its own sheet.**

- **If the three teams select . . .**

  The same space, that space is marked by the facilitator and shown to all teams. This ends the round of play.

  Three different spaces, this ends the round of play.

  Two different spaces, the teams "send" virtual messages to the other two teams. Continue play of round.

- **Continue play in this fashion until there is a mark on three spaces in a row on the Master Game Sheet.**

Virtual X-Change

Use this sheet to track the spaces selected by the three teams by:

- Comparing the numerical selections with your team Game Sheet copies.

- Recording the three selections on your own copies of the team Game Sheets.

If the three selections occur in the same space, mark the appropriate space on the flip chart as well as on this Master Game Sheet. This ends the round.

If NONE of the three spaces match, this ends the round.

If two of the spaces MATCH, have teams meet and then share one set of virtual messages.

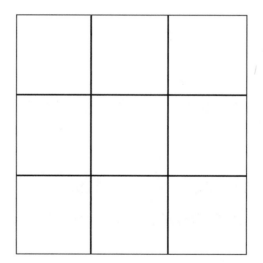

Virtual X-Change.

Select a space and then inform the facilitator of the space number using one of your Message Sheets.

1	2	3
4	5	6
7	8	9

Virtual X-Change..

Select a space and then inform the facilitator of the space number using one of your Message Sheets.

1	4	7
2	5	8
3	6	9

Virtual X-Change...

Select a space and then inform the facilitator of the space number using one of
your Message Sheets.

A	B	C
D	E	F
G	H	I

GAME SHEET FOR
Virtual X-Change....

Select a space and then inform the facilitator of the space number using one of your Message Sheets.

A	D	G
B	E	H
C	F	I

MESSAGE SHEETS FOR
Virtual X-Change

· ·

Virtual Message: Team _____

Round ___

Virtual Message: Team _____

Round ___

Virtual Message: Team _____

Round ___

Virtual Message: Team _____

Round ___

Virtual Message: Team _____

Round ___

Virtual Message: Team _____

Round ___

Virtual Message: Team _____

Round ___

Virtual Message: Team _____

Round ___

About the Authors

Steve Sugar is a teacher who uses interactive games in his management courses at the University of Maryland Baltimore County (UMBC) and a writer of games that focus on a variety of topics in a dynamic learning atmosphere.

Steve has created interactive game designs for the following Jossey-Bass/Pfeiffer books: *Games That Teach* (1998); *Games That Teach Teams* (2000); *Primary Games* (2002); and *Retreats That Work* (2002).

He has also contributed chapters to *The ASTD Handbook of Instructional Technology* (1993) and *The ASTD Handbook of Training Design and Delivery* (1999), as well as the stand-alone game systems, including *QUIZO, X-O Cise,* and the *Management 2000* board game.

Steve has served as editor-contributor to three ASTD INFO-LINE publications and has contributed learning designs to the *Team and Organization Development Sourcebook, The Pfeiffer Annual, Creative New Employee Orientation Programs,* and *The Active Manager's Tool Kit.*

Steve has been featured in articles on learning design published by *Personnel Journal, Training & Development,* and *Training* magazine, as well as *The Baltimore Sun.*

Steve's past experience includes two military tours in Vietnam and stints as a training officer for the Bureau of Engraving and Printing and the Department of Health and Human Services.

Steve has a master's degree from the George Washington University and a bachelor of arts in economics from Bucknell University.

During nearly thirty years as a program manager, team leader, trainer, adjunct professor, and managerial practitioner, **Carol Willett** has served in the Department of State, United States Air Force, Central Intelligence Agency, University of Virginia, Brookings Institution, Federal Executive Institute, and the General Accounting Office (GAO). During a five-year stint in the corporate sector, she served as vice president for innovation and learning in a small startup dedicated to helping multinationals operate across time and space as members of virtual teams. Currently chief learning officer at GAO, Carol is responsible for ensuring continuity of operations by promoting knowledge transfer throughout the organization.

Carol has authored or coauthored numerous books and articles on academic ethics, the process of privatization in Africa, virtual collaboration, career development strategies, and the use of games to support workplace learning. Her published works include "Academic Ethics," in *To Improve the Academy* (Professional and Organizational Development Network for Higher Education, 1994); *Successful Negotiations: The Key to Privatization in Zambia* (Ostrer & Associates, 1996); "Developing Virtual Teams," in *Organizational Development Yearbook* (McGraw-Hill, 1999); "Readiness for Virtual Collaboration," in *Organizational Development Yearbook* (McGraw-Hill, 2000); "Aligning Organizations for Virtual Teams," in *Organizational Development Yearbook* (McGraw-Hill, 2001); "Shifting the Power Equation Through Knowledge Sharing," in *Knowledge Management: Classic and Contemporary Works* (MIT Press, 2001); *TeamSmart Tool for Team Development* (MasteryWorks, 2001); and "Getting Ready for Virtuality," in *Rewiring the Organization* (Pfeiffer, 2002).

Carol has a master's degree from American University and the National Training Laboratory in Organization Development, a master's degree in international relations from Troy State University, and a bachelor of arts degree in international relations from American University. She is certified as a team facilitator, coach, and master trainer.

How to Use the CD-ROM

- ## SYSTEM REQUIREMENTS

    PC with Microsoft Windows 98SE or later

    Mac with Apple OS version 8.6 or later

- ## USING THE CD WITH WINDOWS

    To view the items located on the CD, follow these steps:

    1. Insert the CD into your computer's CD-ROM drive.

    2. A window appears with the following options:

        Contents: Allows you to view the files included on the CD-ROM.

        Software: Allows you to install useful software from the CD-ROM.

        Links: Displays a hyperlinked page of websites.

        Author: Displays a page with information about the author(s).

        Contact Us: Displays a page with information on contacting the publisher or author.

        Help: Displays a page with information on using the CD.

        Exit: Closes the interface window.

If you do not have autorun enabled, or if the autorun window does not appear, follow these steps to access the CD:

1. Click Start → Run.

2. In the dialog box that appears, type d: <\\><\\> start.exe, where d is the letter of your CD-ROM drive. This brings up the autorun window described in the preceding set of steps.

3. Choose the desired option from the menu. (See Step 2 in the preceding list for a description of these options.)

● IN CASE OF TROUBLE

If you experience difficulty using the CD-ROM, please follow these steps:

1. Make sure your hardware and systems configurations conform to the systems requirements noted under "System Requirements" above.

2. Review the installation procedure for your type of hardware and operating system. It is possible to reinstall the software if necessary.

To speak with someone in Product Technical Support, call 800-762-2974 or 317-572-3994 Monday through Friday from 8:30 A.M. to 5:00 P.M. EST. You can also contact Product Technical Support and get support information through our website at www.wiley.com/techsupport.

Before calling or writing, please have the following information available:

- Type of computer and operating system.

- Any error messages displayed.

- Complete description of the problem.

It is best if you are sitting at your computer when making the call.

Pfeiffer Publications Guide

This guide is designed to familiarize you with the various types of Pfeiffer publications. The formats section describes the various types of products that we publish; the methodologies section describes the many different ways that content might be provided within a product. We also provide a list of the topic areas in which we publish.

FORMATS

In addition to its extensive book-publishing program, Pfeiffer offers content in an array of formats, from fieldbooks for the practitioner to complete, ready-to-use training packages that support group learning.

FIELDBOOK Designed to provide information and guidance to practitioners in the midst of action. Most fieldbooks are companions to another, sometimes earlier, work, from which its ideas are derived; the fieldbook makes practical what was theoretical in the original text. Fieldbooks can certainly be read from cover to cover. More likely, though, you'll find yourself bouncing around following a particular theme, or dipping in as the mood, and the situation, dictate.

HANDBOOK A contributed volume of work on a single topic, comprising an eclectic mix of ideas, case studies, and best practices sourced by practitioners and experts in the field.

An editor or team of editors usually is appointed to seek out contributors and to evaluate content for relevance to the topic. Think of a handbook not as a ready-to-eat meal, but as a cookbook of ingredients that enables you to create the most fitting experience for the occasion.

RESOURCE Materials designed to support group learning. They come in many forms: a complete, ready-to-use exercise (such as a game); a comprehensive resource on one topic (such as conflict management) containing a variety of methods and approaches; or a collection of like-minded activities (such as icebreakers) on multiple subjects and situations.

TRAINING PACKAGE An entire, ready-to-use learning program that focuses on a particular topic or skill. All packages comprise a guide for the facilitator/trainer and a workbook for the participants. Some packages are supported with additional media—such as video—or learning aids, instruments, or other devices to help participants understand concepts or practice and develop skills.

- *Facilitator/trainer's guide* Contains an introduction to the program, advice on how to organize and facilitate the learning event, and step-by-step instructor notes. The guide also contains copies of presentation materials—handouts, presentations, and overhead designs, for example—used in the program.

- *Participant's workbook* Contains exercises and reading materials that support the learning goal and serves as a valuable reference and support guide for participants in the weeks and months that follow the learning event. Typically, each participant will require his or her own workbook.

ELECTRONIC CD-ROMs and web-based products transform static Pfeiffer content into dynamic, interactive experiences. Designed to take advantage of the searchability, automation, and ease-of-use that technology provides, our e-products bring convenience and immediate accessibility to your workspace.

METHODOLOGIES

CASE STUDY A presentation, in narrative form, of an actual event that has occurred inside an organization. Case studies are not prescriptive, nor are they used to prove a point; they are designed to develop critical analysis and decision-making skills. A case study has a specific time frame, specifies a sequence of events, is narrative in structure, and contains a plot structure—an issue (what should be/have been done?). Use case studies when the goal is to enable participants to apply previously learned theories to the circumstances in the case, decide what is pertinent, identify the real issues, decide what should have been done, and develop a plan of action.

ENERGIZER A short activity that develops readiness for the next session or learning event. Energizers are most commonly used after a break or lunch to stimulate or refocus the group. Many involve some form of physical activity, so they are a useful way to counter post-lunch lethargy. Other uses include transitioning from one topic to another, where "mental" distancing is important.

EXPERIENTIAL LEARNING ACTIVITY (ELA) A facilitator-led intervention that moves participants through the learning cycle from experience to application (also known as a Structured Experience). ELAs are carefully thought-out designs in which there is a definite learning purpose and intended outcome. Each step—everything that participants do during the activity—facilitates the accomplishment of the stated goal. Each ELA includes complete instructions for facilitating the intervention and a clear statement of goals, suggested group size and timing, materials required, an explanation of the process, and, where appropriate, possible variations to the activity. (For more detail on Experiential Learning Activities, see the Introduction to the *Reference Guide to Handbooks and Annuals*, 1999 edition, Pfeiffer, San Francisco.)

GAME A group activity that has the purpose of fostering team spirit and togetherness in addition to the achievement of a pre-stated goal. Usually contrived—undertaking a desert expedition, for example—this type of learning method offers an engaging means for participants to demonstrate and practice business and interpersonal skills. Games are effective for team building and personal development mainly because the goal is subordinate to the process—the means through which participants reach decisions, collaborate, communicate, and generate trust and understanding. Games often engage teams in "friendly" competition.

ICEBREAKER A (usually) short activity designed to help participants overcome initial anxiety in a training session and/or to acquaint the participants with one another. An icebreaker can be a fun activity or can be tied to specific topics or training goals. While a useful tool in itself, the icebreaker comes into its own in situations where tension or resistance exists within a group.

INSTRUMENT A device used to assess, appraise, evaluate, describe, classify, and summarize various aspects of human behavior. The term used to describe an instrument depends primarily on its format and purpose. These terms include *survey, questionnaire, inventory, diagnostic,* and *poll.* Some uses of instruments include providing instrumental feedback to group members, studying here-and-now processes or functioning within a group, manipulating group composition, and evaluating outcomes of training and other interventions.

Instruments are popular in the training and HR field because, in general, more growth can occur if an individual is provided with a method for focusing specifically on his or her own behavior. Instruments also are used to obtain information that will serve as a basis for change and to assist in workforce planning efforts.

Paper-and-pencil tests still dominate the instrument landscape with a typical package comprising a facilitator's guide, which offers advice on administering the instrument and interpreting the collected data, and an initial set of instruments. Additional instruments are available separately. Pfeiffer, though, is investing heavily in e-instruments. Electronic instrumentation provides effortless distribution and, for larger groups particularly, offers advantages over paper-and-pencil tests in the time it takes to analyze data and provide feedback.

LECTURETTE A short talk that provides an explanation of a principle, model, or process that is pertinent to the participants' current learning needs. A lecturette is intended to establish a common language bond between the trainer and the participants by providing a mutual frame of reference. Use a lecturette as an introduction to a group activity or event, as an interjection during an event, or as a handout.

MODEL A graphic depiction of a system or process and the relationship among its elements. Models provide a frame of reference and something more tangible, and more easily remembered, than a verbal explanation. They also give participants something to "go on," enabling them to track their own progress as they experience the dynamics, processes, and relationships being depicted in the model.

ROLE PLAY A technique in which people assume a role in a situation/scenario: a customer service rep in an angry-customer exchange, for example. The way in which the role is approached is then discussed and feedback is offered. The role play is often repeated using a different approach and/or incorporating changes made based on feedback received. In other words, role playing is a spontaneous interaction involving realistic behavior under artificial (and safe) conditions.

SIMULATION A methodology for understanding the interrelationships among components of a system or process. Simulations differ from games in that they test or use a model that depicts or mirrors some aspect of reality in form, if not necessarily in content. Learning occurs by studying the effects of change on one or more factors of the model. Simulations are commonly used to test hypotheses about what happens in a system—often referred to as "what if?" analysis—or to examine best-case/worst-case scenarios.

THEORY A presentation of an idea from a conjectural perspective. Theories are useful because they encourage us to examine behavior and phenomena through a different lens.

TOPICS

The twin goals of providing effective and practical solutions for workforce training and organization development and meeting the educational needs of training and human resource professionals shape Pfeiffer's publishing program. Core topics include the following:

Leadership & Management

Communication & Presentation

Coaching & Mentoring

Training & Development

E-Learning

Teams & Collaboration

OD & Strategic Planning

Human Resources

Consulting

What will you find on pfeiffer.com?

- The best in workplace performance solutions for training and HR professionals

- Downloadable training tools, exercises, and content

- Web-exclusive offers

- Training tips, articles, and news

- Seamless on-line ordering

- Author guidelines, information on becoming a Pfeiffer Affiliate, and much more

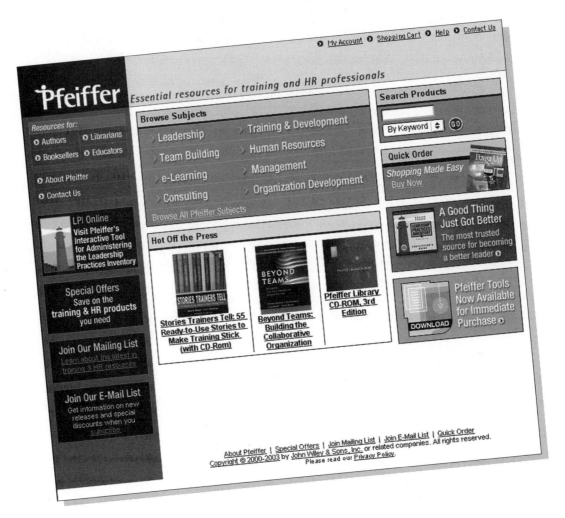

Discover more at www.pfeiffer.com

Customer Care

Have a question, comment, or suggestion? Contact us! We value your feedback and we want to hear from you.

For questions about this or other Pfeiffer products, you may contact us by:

E-mail: **customer@wiley.com**

Mail: **Customer Care Wiley/Pfeiffer**
10475 Crosspoint Blvd.
Indianapolis, IN 46256

Phone: **(U.S.) 800-274-4434** (Outside the U.S.: 317-572-3985)

Fax: **(U.S.) 800-569-0443** (Outside the U.S.: 317-572-4002)

To order additional copies of this title or to browse other Pfeiffer products, visit us online at **www.pfeiffer.com**.

For **Technical Support** questions call **800-762-2974**.

For authors guidelines, log on to www.pfeiffer.com and click on "Resources for Authors."

If you are . . .

A **college bookstore, a professor, an instructor, or work in higher education** and you'd like to place an order or request an exam copy, please contact jbreview@wiley.com.

A **general retail bookseller** and you'd like to establish an account or speak to a local sales representative, contact Melissa Grecco at 201-748-6267 or mgrecco@wiley.com.

An **exclusively online bookseller**, contact Amy Blanchard at 530-756-9456 or ablanchard @wiley.com or Jennifer Johnson at 206-568-3883 or jjohnson@wiley.com, both of our Online Sales department.

A **librarian or library representative**, contact John Chambers in our Library Sales department at 201-748-6291 or jchamber@wiley.com.

A **reseller, training company/consultant, or corporate trainer**, contact Charles Regan in our Special Sales department at 201-748-6553 or cregan@wiley.com.

A **specialty retail distributor** (includes specialty gift stores, museum shops, and corporate bulk sales), contact Kim Hendrickson in our Special Sales department at 201-748-6037 or khendric@wiley.com.

Purchasing for the **Federal government**, contact Ron Cunningham in our Special Sales department at 317-572-3053 or rcunning@wiley.com.

Purchasing for a **State or Local government**, contact Charles Regan in our Special Sales department at 201-748-6553 or cregan@wiley.com.